FILMMA
ed
ANTH(

Designing for the Movies

The Memoirs of Laurence Irving

Laurence Irving

Filmmakers Series, No. 121

The Scarecrow Press, Inc.
Lanham, Maryland • Toronto • Oxford
2005

SCARECROW PRESS, INC.

Published in the United States of America
by Scarecrow Press, Inc.
A wholly owned subsidary of
The Rowman & Littlefield Publishing Group, Inc.
4501 Forbes Boulevard, Suite 200, Lanham, Maryland 20706
www.scarecrowpress.com

PO Box 317
Oxford
OX2 9RU, UK

British Library Cataloguing in Publication Information Available

Library of Congress Cataloging-in-Publication Data

Irving, Laurence, 1897–
    Designing for the movies : the memoirs of Laurence Irving / Laurence Irving.
        p. cm. — (Filmmakers series ; no. 121)
    Includes index.
    ISBN 0-8108-5671-9 (pbk. : alk. paper)
    1. Irving, Laurence, 1897– . 2. Motion picture set designers—United States—
Biography. I. Title. II. Series.
PN1998.3.I76A3 2005
791.4302'5'092—dc22   2005007960

∞™ The paper used in this publication meets the minimum requirements
of American National Standard for Information Sciences—Permanence of
Paper for Printed Library Materials, ANSI/NISO Z39.48-1992.
Manufactured in the United States of America.

CONTENTS

EDITOR'S FOREWORD

Laurence Irving (1897–1988) came from a prominent British theatrical family, the grandson of the legendary Sir Henry Irving (whom he affectionately refers to as "the antique") and the son of actor H. B. Irving and his actress wife Dorothea Baird. However, unlike his forebears, Laurence chose not to enter the acting profession but gained an international reputation as an artist, set designer, and art director. He designed the sets for the original Canterbury Cathedral production of T. S. Eliot's *Murder in the Cathedral* (later used for the original London presentation), as well as plays by Frederick Lonsdale, J. B. Priestley, and Ben Travers. Among the actors with whom he was closely associated are John Clements, Michael Redgrave, and Donald Wolfit.

Two of his autobiographical works were published (along with a number of books for which he provided illustrations), but this present volume is taken from an unpublished autobiography, *Abiding Curiosity*, documenting Irving's life and career from 1919 through 1939. The new book, *Designing for the Movies*, as its title suggests, covers Irving's career in Hollywood, working with Douglas Fairbanks on *The Iron Mask* and with Fairbanks and Mary Pickford on *The Taming of the Shrew*, and his work in the United Kingdom on *Moonlight Sonata*, starring Ignaz Paderewski, and the Gabriel Pascal productions from the plays of George Bernard Shaw, most notably *Pygmalion*. It offers a unique insight into the early career of Hollywood's most famous art director, William Cameron Menzies, and documents the working methods of Maurice Leloir, the original illustrator of the novels of Alexandre Dumas, whom Fairbanks brought to Hollywood to work on *The Iron Mask*.

Laurence Irving was as good a writer as he was a designer, and the reader will quickly discover that he provides brilliant word portraits of those with whom he came into contact. Not only does he make Fairbanks and Pickford come alive as personalities, but he is equally magnificent in his descriptions of "lesser" individuals such as producer Joseph M. Schenck.

Aside from the films discussed here, it should be noted that Laurence Irving not only designed but also co-produced the 1947 feature, *Uncle Silas* (released in the United States as *The Inheritance*), starring Jean Simmons and

Katina Paxinou, and written by Irving's longtime friend, Ben Travers. After *Uncle Silas*, Irving spent three years researching and writing the definitive biography of Henry Irving. Laurence conceived this writing project as the story of one hundred years of the Irving theatrical family. The HI biography was the first volume, covering his life from 1838 to 1905. The second volume, *The Successors*, told the story of HI's two sons, Harry and Laurence, both actors and writers, from the moment in 1871 when their father walked out of his wife's life, leaving her to look after the boys' upbringing to HI's funeral in Westminster Abbey. The third volume, *The Precarious Crust*, followed the sons' careers and marriages and the author's early years and service as a fighter pilot in WWI. The book ends with HI's death in 1919. The final volume to complete this century project in 1938 remained in manuscript form but has now been put together and published under the title *Designing for the Movies: The Memoirs of Laurence Irving*.

In order not to lose track of Laurence Irving's life and career outside of film, his son, John H. B. Irving, provides linking commentary and an introduction. The epilogue to this book is taken from Laurence Irving's account of his five years in the Royal Air Force during World War II (for which he was awarded the OBE), *Great Interruption*, originally published in 1983 by Airlife.

Anthony Slide, Series Editor

INTRODUCTION

John H. B. Irving

My father, Laurence, was born in London on April 11, 1897. He was the first child of Harry and Dorothea Irving, both in the early years of their acting careers. Harry was known professionally as H. B. Irving. His father was the famous actor Sir Henry Irving, who, two years before, had become the first professional actor to receive a knighthood from Queen Victoria. Henry was a sick man at the end of a celebrated career, but his dedication to the art of theatre and his Lyceum Company made any thought of a retirement impossible. Harry had a younger brother Laurence, who was also a dedicated actor. As the two emerged from under the formidable shadow of their illustrious father, they both became very close in their difficult predicament.

Queen Victoria died in 1901, and, in October 1905, while on tour with his Company in Northern England, Henry Irving, following a performance of *Becket* at the Theatre Royal, Bradford, collapsed and died seated on a chair in the lobby of his hotel. His grandson Laurence, then aged eight, remembered attending the magnificent funeral in Westminster Abbey with his grandmother, Lady Florence Irving. She had been estranged from her husband for thirty years following a caustic remark she had made after the first night of his first real London success—*The Bells*. At his funeral Florence was in no mourning mood. She watched the stately coffin, knowing that there was no body inside—only a casket of ashes. Henry's burial place, set beneath a small inscribed floor stone in the sacred "Poets' Corner" of the Abbey, was too crowded for anything larger.

Dorothea's family, the Bairds, lived in Oxford. She was the youngest of six sisters and grew up in a university atmosphere. She enjoyed acting in school plays and later joined an amateur dramatic society. Her beauty led to leading parts and soon her life ambition centered on a theatrical career. Harry and Laurence Irving lived in London with their mother, liberally supported by her estranged husband. He preferred his sons to have conventional private educations leading hopefully to Harry becoming a lawyer and Laurence a diplomat. In 1890 the Lyceum Company was in financial

difficulties, and Henry Irving could no longer support his sons so generously. He wrote to Florence suggesting that careers on the stage might be
the best solution, a change in their future both boys welcomed.

Harry joined a repertory company run by Ben Greet, of which Dorothea
Baird was also a member. The two were attracted to each other. Harry
then left the company for another offer. They wrote frequently to each
other. Harry's letters have survived and they chart a growing affection.
Then Dolly, as she was known, was cast in a leading role in a new play
Trilby, which had had great success in New York. It was the story of an
artist's model who falls into the hands of an unscrupulous German musi-
cian, Svengali, a man with hypnotic powers. A leading English actor, Herbert Beerbohm Tree, played the part in the new London production. The
first night was a great success, and Dolly became an immediate star.
Harry continued his tours round the country taking on many parts, few
of which drew any praise. Their correspondence continued. Eventually he
proposed to her. An interview with Dolly's barrister father started an in-
terfamily round of questions and answers. On July 20, 1896, Dolly and
Harry were married in London's St. Pancras Church before a congregation of hundreds of relations and members of the acting profession. The
reception was held at a house in Tavistock Square. A large crowd outside
shouted "Trilby, Trilby!" Bride and groom came out onto the balcony to
wave to those below. The event was widely reported in the press. The
honeymoon was spent at Bamburgh on the coast of Northumberland, the
county from where the Baird family originated. My father was born in
London on April 11 of the following year.

His early childhood was spent in an apartment in Bloomsbury, the intellectual centre of London near the British Library and the British Museum. Access to library records was essential, for Harry's legal studies at
Oxford had sparked his lifelong interest in criminology, and, by this time,
he was already working on his study of the life of the controversial
seventeenth-century character Judge Jefferies. Harry had also been
elected to the famous Garrick Club. Members were leading figures from
the theatre, the law, and national politics, and Henry Irving had a reserved seat at the club's dining table. Harry and Dolly's theatre work continued, and their son's needs were met by a nurse called Ada. In 1904
Dolly had a daughter, Elizabeth, and brother and sister developed a bond
that held for the rest of their long lives. Then the time came when Harry
and Dolly started their own theatre company, which toured the country
and eventually abroad. The Baird family in Oxford welcomed the two
youngsters whenever these tours became too long. Laurence and Elizabeth relished the Baird family atmosphere. In September 1912, Dolly
heard from a former Lyceum Company actor, Frank Tyars, that a property
was on the market in the Kentish town of Whitstable, near where he and

other theatre people had holiday homes. This was the Black Windmill with three acres of land and a miller's cottage. The disused mill stood prominently on the top of Borstal Hill overlooking the town, its port, and the North Sea. Harry agreed that a country home one hour's train ride away from London would be a great family asset. Dolly's father had recently given one thousand pounds to each of his daughters, and this gift provided the means for the restoration of the mill and its cottage.

My father's schooling took him to a private preparatory school in South Dorset near the town of Swanage. Its name was Durnford, and it was set on the high hills looking down on the sea coast of the English Channel. Its greatest asset was its headmaster, Tom Pellatt, an Oxford graduate and a good friend of the Bairds. His wife, Nell, complemented her husband's talents. They were both keen theatregoers, and Laurence had the happiest memories of his time at that school. He became fascinated with the developing story of manned flight, and he designed and built model aircraft in the school's workshop. During this time Harry and Dolly took their company on tour to Australia and New Zealand. Dolly was torn between her love for her husband and her ties to her children, however well their needs could be met in her absence. While the company was performing in Melbourne, she had a complete breakdown and had to leave the cast. She later tried to resume her roles, but this proved impossible. It was the end of their theatrical partnership. In Durban the news arrived from England that she had been elected to the St. Pancras Board of Guardians, the group in charge of infant welfare in that part of London. Her participation in this work became her central concern for the rest of her life. Harry's life took a new turn when he was persuaded by his solicitor to take advantage of the offer of the Savoy Theatre on a twenty-one-year lease on very attractive terms. He became, therefore, more an impresario than an actor manager. He also ensured a good income for his family in increasingly difficult times.

When time came for Laurence to move on to a private "public school," he was less fortunate. His parents, on Tom Pellatt's advice, decided to send him to Wellington College, a school founded in memory of the duke and his victory over Napoleon at the Battle of Waterloo. Most of its students were sons of military officers. The arts were largely disregarded. The door to Laurence's private room was placarded with a scribbled sign reading "*SON OF A DIRTY ACTOR.*" His time at Wellington was educationally unsuccessful and sad. He left Wellington College as soon as it could be arranged.

In 1914 the family suffered a major tragedy. Harry's brother Laurence, with his actress wife Mabel, had created a touring theatre company. They had been travelling round Canada and had ended a very successful tour in Toronto. Eager to get home, they booked on the liner *Empress of Ireland* which left Montreal on the evening of May 28. That night, in a fog-bound

Gulf of St. Lawrence, the liner was rammed by a heavily loaded coal ship. The damage was fatal, and the liner began to sink. Only four of the many lifeboats were launched. The passenger losses were higher than those of the *Titanic* disaster three years before. Laurence and Mabel's bodies were never found. A few months later, war was declared in Europe.

My father was seventeen years old. He wanted to volunteer for flying training. Harry insisted that he go first to Oxford to study for the university entrance exam, which was duly taken and passed. He returned to London. One evening when Harry was dining at the Garrick Club, he found himself sitting next to a Captain Murray Sueter, director of the Air Department of the Admiralty. He told him of his son's interest in flying. "Just the sort of chap we need," said Sueter. "He should come and see me." To Laurence this was wonderful news. The Admiralty interview went well, and he was given an immediate medical check, which he passed successfully. The next day he went to the leading London tailors, Messrs Gieves & Co, and ordered the regulation uniforms and equipment of an officer in the Royal Naval Air Service (RNAS). He reported to the training airfield at Hendon, just outside London.

The aircraft on which Laurence received his initial training had several similar features to the biplane, which the Wright brothers had been the first to fly under its own power on the beaches of North Carolina eleven years before. Another trainee was the future playwright Ben Travers. Because of Ben's theatre interests he was pointed out a weedy younger recruit with similar connections. "Good God. Is *that* an Irving!" Laurence and Ben became the greatest of friends for the rest of their lives. Prospects for survival in their line of business were slim. Any flying was extremely hazardous. To fly into battle with no parachute in a "stringbag" machine was an almost certain death sentence. Laurence came through several crashes during the rest of his training. He was then posted to an airfield behind the British front line in Belgium. He won his first combat with an enemy plane, but soon after he himself was shot down onto a no-man's-land area near the coast. He was unwounded and stayed motionless beside his wrecked aircraft until nightfall, when he crawled back safely to friendly trenches. Further operations followed until he was posted home to an airfield in Northern England as a flying instructor. By that time he had mastered the art of flying. He had also received the visual inspiration of moving in three dimensions through beautifully shaped cloud structures—an experience which dominated his first postwar attempts at drawing and painting.

On April 1, 1917, the RNAS was absorbed into the newly formed Royal Air Force. All personnel were given thorough reexaminations. To Laurence's dismay and salvation he was found to have a tubercular gland in his neck, which was overdue for surgical removal. The operation took place in the London Hospital for Officers. The results were successful, though his recovery process was painful and lengthy. The family arranged that he should be looked after in Northumberland at Bamburgh Castle, the home of Lord Armstrong. His sister Elizabeth came with him. There followed a time of deep introspection. Eventually he decided that his future must be that of an artist and painter.

Dolly meanwhile had remained in London. Harry was very ill and needed constant attention. He had developed a fatal kidney disorder. Laurence returned home to London and started studying art at the Royal Academy. His father was confined to his bed. He spent his last days correcting the proofs of his eighth book on criminology and famous criminals. He died on October 17, 1919, at the age of forty-nine with all his family around him.

Laurence returned to his art studies. As Christmas approached, Elizabeth, now fifteen, was invited by a friend, Sylvia Thompson, to join a New Year party at the luxurious home in Surrey of Sir Robert Mond. Laurence was designated to be her chaperon. There was a formal dinner and dance. The girls came in fancy dress. Laurence spotted an attractive latecomer. Her name was Rosalind Woolner. He asked her to dance. By the end of the evening Laurence was certain he had fallen in love. His own appearance was marred by a heavily bandaged throat as he had not been healing properly from his operation.

A few days later he had to return to hospital for another operation. He haemorrhaged seriously. Dolly fulfilled his request that Rosalind, who was serving as a nurse in another hospital, should come and visit him. As Laurence recovered he became Rosalind's best hope of an escape from a difficult stepmother. Marriage possibilities dominated their thoughts. Laurence went to see her father, Hugh Woolner, the son of the Pre-Raphaelite sculptor, Thomas Woolner. Hugh's talents were confined to great personal charm and the desire to advise others on their investments, which usually landed his clients serious losses. He readily approved of his future son-in-law. At that moment one less family mouth to feed was a great help to him financially.

Laurence had received a substantial financial settlement from the Navy, and from 1921 he could count on an allowance from his late father's estate. In September 1920 he was studying at the Byam Shaw School of Art. The following spring, Rosalind and he were married at St. Pancras Church. The generous wedding present from Robert Mond was spent on a small car, which took them down to a camping honeymoon in Cornwall. They drove back to Kent and settled down in the miller's cottage overlooked by the Black Windmill. The family's only connection now with the stage was Elizabeth. She joined a company run by James Fagan and played Titania in a well-reviewed Christmas production of *A Midsummer Night's Dream* at the Court Theatre.

Laurence continued his arts studies at the Royal Academy School in Burlington House. He responded enthusiastically to two of his teachers, Charles Ricketts and Charles Shannon. They were not only instructors, but also weekly hosts to a group of young Academy students with food and good conversation in abundance. In the year before he died, Harry had allowed his son's name to be put forward for election to the Garrick Club. The election page with his name was covered with signatures of many members, and he was elected without opposition. As Laurence later put it, "No doubt the lives of many members like myself were influenced by chance encounters in the club's fateful precincts."

As 1920 progressed and Laurence's studies continued, things were happening at the Black Windmill. Rosalind was expecting their first child. Dolly had come into some more Baird money, which she spent on restoring the structure of the windmill and creating in its octagonal first floor a fine artist's studio for her son. She constructed for herself a thatched cottage on the southern edge of the garden. Laurence sought to increase his income by entering the Prix de Rome competition. Choosing the engravings section, he and Rosalind installed a secondhand lithographic press on the ground floor of the windmill. Prints of his artwork, influenced by the sinister shades of Frank Brangwyn, had to be etched and printed after dark. Even though his entry to the engravings section of the competition was the only one submitted, no prize was forthcoming.

Laurence's attention was next drawn to Whitstable's harbour and boat building yards. The town was nationally famous for oyster fishing, so the building and repair of boats was an essential part of the local economy. Boatyard scenes became fine subjects for Laurence's watercolours. His first canvas to be accepted by the annual exhibition at London's Royal Academy was of a collier brig under repair. The picture was sold. As Laurence was painting this picture, he saw a derelict twenty-four-foot lifeboat. He bought the hulk for five pounds and arranged for it to be dragged up Borstal Hill by a steam traction engine. It was placed in the mill's garden, there to be converted into a sailing boat to take him and Rosalind across the English Channel to Calais, the gateway to many miles of inland waterways. Work began during the winter as Rosalind's womb grew to full size.

On March 22, 1921, Pamela Mary was born. Her name was painted on the stern of the refurbished lifeboat. That summer, Laurence and a fellow Royal Academy student sailed the *Pamela Mary* to France and then inland up the waterways to Belgium and Holland. There were many waterside subjects to be sketched and painted, and the changing weather gave him a variety of backgrounds. The voyage home was uneventful. That winter he worked on the material in preparation for his first London exhibition at the Fine Arts Society. The proceeds were sufficient to cover the costs of his boat and the expedition. His next project started with a meeting at the publishers Methuen & Co. Its chairman, E. V. Lucas, had been a great friend of Laurence's father, and he wanted Laurence to illustrate a book that an American was writing about the River Thames. The plan was for Laurence to steer his boat up the river to Lechlade, where the writer, Frank Morley, would join him. They would then live on the boat and travel down the Thames as each plied his own trade with words and pictures. Frank arrived at Lechlade station loaded with suitcases, a ditty bag, and a portable typewriter. He and Laurence shook hands and began a lasting friendship. Their downriver voyage was most productive. Frank had been a Rhodes Scholar at Oxford. His knowledge of the literature of the sea was enormous. Laurence listened and learned from their evening conversations and was introduced to the wonderful nautical tales penned by the sixteenth-century author Richard Hakluyt. Frank Morley's *River Thames* was beautifully published with sixteen watercolour plates.

Laurence's next project was an edited version of *Hakluyt—Voyages & Discoveries of the English* with his own illustrations done in a vigorous black-and-white style to suit the period. The book's foreword is dedicated to his newly born son John and speculates on what thoughts were going through his infant mind as he explored the carpet on the floor of his father's studio. The publisher was Charles Evans of Heinemann, whom Laurence had met at the Garrick Club. He had heard of the Hakluyt project and suggested that he should be its publisher. The substantial demand for the book resulted in a second edition. As a result, Evans was happy to back Laurence's next book idea, a limited edition of the recent verse play by the poet John Masefield titled *Philip the King* with Laurence's illustrations and decorations in a style similar to the Hakluyt book. Both works covered the same historical period. An edition of 250 copies was personally signed by author and artist, and surviving copies are now valuable collectors' items.

Up to this point Laurence had not considered theatre design to be within his artistic ambitions. From childhood he knew that all aspects of theatrical production were prime family concerns. He had been taken to many shows and saw all that went on to create the illusion of reality on the stage. He knew how the mechanisms of scenery worked and how acting areas were delineated by lines of sight from the auditorium and the arrangement of lighting. Finally he understood how a designer's clear plans and sketches determined the success with which the theatre craftsmen built what was required. So it happened on another Garrick occasion that Laurence was introduced to Harold Fraser Simpson, a Scottish lord, who was also a composer. He was working on the score of a new revue about to be produced at London's Vaudeville Theatre under the title *Vaudeville Vanities*. He suggested to the producer that Laurence be asked to design sets and costumes for two scenes. The suggestion was put into effect. Laurence returned to Whitstable to give Rosalind the exciting news. The revue was a success, and Laurence's work received excellent reviews from the critics.

This improvement in his prospects allowed Laurence to set in motion the design and building of a new house attached to the Black Windmill. For some years the miller's cottage had needed major repairs, but its size was insufficient for the growing family. The architect Arthur Knapp-Fisher created a three story L-shaped house clad in brick and weather boarding with red and white Dutch-style window shutters that contrasted well with the towering black mill structure.

That summer Laurence spotted another temptation in a Whitstable boat-yard. It was a regular fishing boat, an oyster smack, more substantial than the *Pamela Mary* lifeboat and better suited to his plans for a further paint-ing expedition to the Dutch waterways. The new boat was refitted and en-dowed also with the *Pamela Mary* name. Charles Evans heard about his re-newed interest in painting scenes in Holland. He suggested that Laurence should work on a new illustrated book based on his Dutch adventures. Rosalind and their one-year-old son came out to join the *Pamela Mary*.

Another old Garrick family friend, Eddie Knoblock, enjoyed tales of this voyage. Born an American and educated at Harvard, he had em-barked on an acting career in New York. There he met another young ac-tor named Douglas Fairbanks, and they became great friends. They headed off in opposite directions, Douglas to California and films, Eddie to England and a successful career as a dramatist, but they kept in touch. Eddie had studied French history and the culture of the reign of Louis XIV. He received a call to help Douglas with the scenery and costumes of his 1921 silent film, *The Three Musketeers*. Eddie's next job was to prepare a film script of his recent play, an oriental fantasy titled *Kismet*, which Douglas retitled *The Thief of Bagdad*. Both films built the basis of the Fair-banks film reputation. When Douglas started talking about plans to de-sign a film based on Alexandre Dumas's *The Man in The Iron Mask*, Eddie must have given him the name of a young painter in England with the-atrical connections.

The *Pamela Mary* returned safely to Whitstable, and Laurence went to work on the new book, *Windmills and Waterways*. E. V. Lucas came down to stay at the Black Windmill to attend Canterbury Cricket Week, an an-nual competition and festival with special theatre shows. Laurence's sis-ter Elizabeth was now a professional actress and was appearing in the part of Trilby—the role that launched her mother, Dolly, into stardom and she, of course, was there to assist her daughter. Later that year Laurence had a second exhibition of his paintings at the Fine Arts Society, which in-cluded costume designs and the originals of his book illustrations. The

number of sales was encouraging. In the New Year he received an invitation from the Dean of Canterbury, George Bell, to call on him to discuss a
matter on which he needed his advice. The Dean had asked John Masefield to write a play that could be produced within the cathedral as an act
of worship matching the traditional medieval mystery plays. It was a bold
idea, but he had to persuade his conventional cathedral staff that it would
be suitable for its setting. The play had two acts. In the first the
Archangels tried to persuade the Spirit of Christ not to attempt an incar-
nation into so wicked a world. The second act told the story of the Nativ-
ity and the Adoration of the Kings and Shepherds. The composer, Gustav
Holst, was writing the accompanying music. Laurence suggested that
Charles Ricketts, who lived nearby with his friend Charles Shannon at
Chilham Castle, should be asked to design the costumes and supervise
the pageantry. The Dean asked if this was a real possibility. Laurence had
studied with Ricketts and assured Bell that he could persuade him. From
that moment on, Laurence became deeply involved in the annual Canterbury Drama Festivals. George Bell and his wife, Hetty, became great family friends. After John Masefield's *The Coming of Christ*, more new plays
were commissioned, the most famous of which was T. S. Eliot's *Murder in
the Cathedral* about the life and death of Thomas à Becket. The plays were
financed by private donations, with many donors taking minor parts and
professional actors in the leading roles.

The Coming of Christ was played on a special stage constructed in the
Cathedral's Chapter House. There were four performances to a total audience of 6,000. Many people came down from London. The critics were
divided on the merits of the play and the players but unanimous in praise
of Dean Bell's courageous gesture. The happy ending of this first production was the prelude to the most exciting turn of events in the whole of
Laurence's life.

ONE

After the last performance George Bell dismissed us with his blessing. It was after midnight when Rosalind and I returned to our home. Reaction had set in. The prolonged farewells at the deanery had left us physically and emotionally exhausted. As we stumbled upstairs on our way to bed, I saw a telegram lying on a chest in the hall. Belated good wishes, I thought—they could wait till morning. For some reason or other I had to go downstairs again, and so in passing I opened it.

WOULD LIKE TO SEE YOU 9 A.M. TOMORROW HYDE PARK HOTEL WITH EXAMPLES OF YOUR WORK

—DOUGLAS FAIRBANKS

We were roused from our stupor. Here was a bolt from Olympus, for Doug Fairbanks and Mary Pickford were as gods in the eyes of their global public. What could this portend? It was already tomorrow. The summons must be obeyed. In a daze I gathered up a portfolio of such work as I thought could conceivably interest so great a film producer. There seemed little enough. We lay sleepless in speculation of what the day now dawning would bring. For an hour or two I passed out in sweet oblivion. The tension of the last few days was relaxed. I left my wife, Rosalind, still sleepy-eyed to catch the early train to London.

I reached the Hyde Park Hotel with ten minutes to spare—time to collect my wits for the coming interview. While I patrolled Knightsbridge in the sunshine, I suspected that Eddie Knoblock had spoken of me to Fairbanks. I should certainly have sought his advice, but he was abroad and anyway there had been no time to do so. Would I be faced with the beaming bounding embodiment of D'Artagnan, Robin Hood, and Zorro—his ebullient self—or a polite impresario fulfilling a boring obligation to a friend?

At the stroke of nine I entered the hotel. At the name of Fairbanks every functionary in the foyer was bowing to me, and a clearly impressed pageboy showed me to the elevator. The lad rapped on the door of Mr. Fairbanks's suite, announced me, and, having ushered me into the sitting room, abandoned me. Nobody was to be seen. A distant voice, rather high-pitched but welcoming, cried, "Is that you, Mr. Irving? Come right in!"

An open door led to the bedroom. I peered in and, seeing no one there, was about to retreat when the sound of splashing water and a further invitation to come right in drew me towards the adjoining bathroom. And there in the bath was my and the world's make-believe hero, as brown as a Polynesian, grinning and radiating a friendliness that instantly put me at ease.

"Sit down!" he commanded with a gesture that implied a wide choice of easy chairs and sofas. There was no choice. Lowering the lid I sat down upon the only seat available. As he floundered in the tub, well aware of my emotional apprehension, he explained rapidly and explicitly the purpose of his telegram. He had heard of my work from Eddie, was eager to see it, and rhapsodised on the wonderful opportunities for artists like myself in moving pictures.

Out of his bath, he dried himself slowly, pausing now and again to stress the limitless scope and social importance of the new medium. I could hardly believe that I was having so intimate a view of the gymnastic genius who, before the eyes of the world, had extricated himself from the deadliest perils that his scriptwriters or he himself could contrive.

He was shorter in stature than I expected—by no means the classic athlete of the Greek ideal. But at forty-five, he was perfectly proportioned according to the delineations of Leonardo da Vinci—an inverted triangle with sides running straight from his broad, muscular shoulders to the apex of his ankles. His trim figure gave him the graceful balance of an all-around athlete. His head was round, and his tanned features were Latin rather than Saxon; his black hair (just beginning to recede), discreet sideburns, and narrow moustache gave him the look of an Iberian aristocrat. As he spoke, he emphasised his phrases by thrusting forward his lower lip like a Hapsburg. Indeed, he may have picked up this mannerism from his friend and admirer King Alfonso of Spain. His vitality and good humour were infectious. The actor in him flamboyantly declaimed that no obstacle in the pursuit of an ideal was insuperable. Most of the successful players I had known had their idiosyncratic vanities. This man, though his acclaim was not to be measured in decibels of applause, had, like Chaplin, won an audience exceeding that of any previous mime. Yet, as I sat fascinated on my lavatory seat, I discerned no conceit in him nor vainglory in his achievement—simply an exuberant confidence in himself as a missionary of a gospel of healthy optimism he could illustrate with romantic parables that breached the barriers of Babel. He may have taken for granted my earlier conversion as a devotee, but at our first meeting he spoke of himself not at all. Whatever he had in mind, I knew that any talents I had were at his disposal.

Later I thought how strange it was that within a month or so I had been enthralled by two men who, though almost opposed in their attitude and beliefs, changed the course of my working life and added a new dimension to my understanding. Respectively, they were the ardent advocates of spiritual well-being and physical health, conceding perhaps that both were necessary to salvation. There must have been a common denominator in their magnetism. It was, I think, the absolute sincerity of their professions of an ideal—a sincerity that is all too rarely encountered in a lifetime—that invoked in me a genetic response inherited from my Uncle Laurence. To equate George Bell and Douglas Fairbanks may seem ridiculously sentimental. Admittedly, the priest endured in his preachment of eternal verities, while the player's convictions waned with the ebbing of his physical energy and his popularity. But, when the tide of their affairs was in the flood, their evangelisms were utterly compatible.

We drifted into the bedroom, and, while he dressed, he told me of his admiration, as a Broadway apprentice, of my grandfather whose Richelieu and Shylock he ranked with Salvini's Othello as incomparable performances. He gave a more faithful imitation of the force and mannerisms of "the antique" than the many and often tedious ones I had been subjected to previously.

Having dressed, nonchalantly and impeccably, he led me to the sitting room where coffee and my portfolio were laid upon the table. He seemed genuinely pleased with my drawings (I realised later that those for *Philip the King* were the most movie-worthy); "Gee! I like that!" punctuated his leisurely perusal of them. As he laid down the last, he turned to me and asked if I would be prepared to join him and Mary in Rome in three days time, sail with them from Naples, and work with them on his next picture—say for six months. Such was the staggering denouement of our brief encounter. Before I had time to consider its implications, he looked over my shoulder (I had my back to the sitting room door) and said, "Before you make up your mind, I think you should have a talk with my business manager."

I turned to find myself looking down into the blue, amiably mocking eyes of the world's sweetheart assessing with frank amusement and a practised scepticism the value of Douglas's latest discovery. Greeting me as warmly as he had done, she said with an air of apology, "I'm afraid that as you have no experience of our medium we can only offer you 250 dollars a week."

The Irish brogue of Gladys Smith was wrapped in the tissue of the American accent Mary Pickford as a child actress had acquired for the stage. The blond ringlets that kept her evergreen in her screen teens were hidden under a cloche hat of the period. Though I, like her millions of admirers, was utterly persuaded of her perpetual adolescence on the screen, face to face with her I had no doubt that the petite, little woman confronting me was a veteran actress and a formidable negotiator who knew her own mind and my worth in terms of her husband's hard-earned cash. For once she overestimated her duty to drive a hard bargain. For by then I had lost my heart to them both. Douglas's pep talk and his flattering intimation that he needed my services had so intoxicated me that I was theirs for the asking; and anyway the salary seemed princely in terms of my then precarious earnings. In five minutes I was pledged to them. They apologised for leaving me so hastily, but they had several appointments before they left London in the afternoon. A representative of United Artists would make all the arrangements for the journey. "Look forward then to seeing you, Laurence, in Rome—Ambassadors Hotel—Saturday." So swiftly had they adopted me. With a pounding heart I asked if I might use their telephone. "Go right ahead!" And they were gone.

Three days later, in proud occupation of my first sleeping car that had all the handy comforts of a yacht's cabin, as the train rattled through the rolling hills of the Pas de Calais, I had at last time to reflect on the scramble of my departure. Rosalind had stoutly insisted that such a chance was not to be missed and made light of caring for the children in my absence. Dolly, mindful of her own dutiful separations from her children, gave moral support to the venture and practical expression of it in the gift of a teddy-bear overcoat (camel's hair teased into pseudofur) to protect me in the variable climates I was committed to; it was the first of its kind to be seen in America, and such was its novelty that I was constantly refusing to sell it for sums that would have kept me in comfort for some time. Nevertheless, to have abandoned my family for six months seemed a betrayal, a feeling sharpened by misgivings that Rosalind's cheerful farewells may have been bravado.

I had a princely reception at the Ambassadors Hotel, Rome, the manager still aglow in the reflected glory of his illustrious guests. A note had been left by Douglas bidding me to follow him to Naples, from where we would embark for New York the next morning. I found too, waiting for me, sleeper tickets for the train that left Rome at midnight. After a sumptuous dinner I left the hotel to find the city plated with silver moonlight. I hailed a fiacre and in dog Latin conveyed to the drowsy driver that for two hours he could be my coachman guide and drive me where he would.

It was an evening of pure magic: clattering over the Ponte San Angelo in the shadow of the fortress tomb and the ramparts from which Benvenuto Cellini with the brio of a Fairbanks had peppered the enemies of his Pope with artillery; emerging from dark narrow streets to see Bellini's colonnade embracing the piazza that lay like a lagoon at the foot of the beetling cliffs of St. Peter; driving round the course of the Piazza Navone where ghostly fountains were tableaux vivants of figures relaxing and re-grouping themselves as I passed them like a potentate reviewing a guard of honour. A crack of the whip, a Roman exhortation to the weary horse, and off we rumbled from one moonlit marvel to another. The Forum might have been a stricken town in the Ypres salient, the Coliseum tow-ering granite crags of a desert island. Later, I came to know Rome well. But I never recaptured the enchantment of that first dreamlike perambu-lation through the veiled magnificence of its antiquity.

Early the next morning I basked in the sunshine on the quay outside the Excelsior Hotel in Naples. Creamy smoke edged with gold poured lazily from the summit of Vesuvius rising through the mists that hid the cities of the plain from view; behind me was the little harbour from which the younger Pliny had sailed in his yacht to rescue his father whose fatal cu-riosity had lured him to his death in Pompeii.

Later, while I was breakfasting, a message from Douglas invited me to join him when I had finished my meal. I found him at the mercy of an Ital-ian professor pressing him to buy a quattrocento panel of a Virgin and Child. Even I doubted its provenance. I winked warningly to Douglas over the professor's shoulder; he acknowledged my signal with another wink of reassurance that he would not be had. Undeterred the scholar-merchant led us by a side door from the hotel and through deserted side streets to the museum—a precautionary route of necessity that would soon be plain to me.

After marveling at various and exquisite Roman artifacts ranging from jewels to surgical instruments, we were accorded the doubtful privilege of a private view of the "black" room, where the dreary and depressing vul-garities of the pornographic decorators of Pompeii were displayed in a semidarkness that gave it an air of shameful secrecy. If there is a purga-tory, its nethermost circle must be the eternal lodging of artists and crafts-men condemned to contemplate forever the debasement of their skills as panderers to a decadent society.

When we returned as surreptitiously to the hotel, I understood the need for subterfuge. Mary was waiting for us among the pyramids of baggage. I could hear the murmuring of an expectant crowd. Through the window I saw the quays thronged as far as one could see with men, women, and children waiting for the revelation of their god and goddess. Later I un-derstood why Italians were Douglas's most ardent fans. Four years ago he had filmed *The Mark of Zorro*, the tale of a Spanish Robin Hood in early California. Since then one cinema in Rome had run it continuously; as one print wore out, another was readied. Our appearance on the steps of the hotel was greeted with a roar of "Zorro! Zorro! Dooglass! Dooglass!" And the women in the crowd gazed upon Mary with reverent adulation as though an effigy of the Virgin was in their midst. In an open car we were wafted, as it were, on a surge of exultant Neapolitans to the gangway of the *Roma*, the new flagship of the Italian trans-Atlantic fleet. Bold and aggressive signature hunters thrust out their cards and photographs. Good-naturedly Douglas and Mary scribbled their ways up the gangway, police close behind them, and with unruffled calm and royal dignity they accepted obeisance and sheaves of flowers from the captain and officials of the line. Yet their duty to the public that was the sinew of their enterprise was not done. From an upper deck they waved farewells to the vast assembly of fans that filled the docks and whose cheers were accompanied by the tooting and booming of ships' sirens. Douglas, who had dined with Mussolini the previous evening, gave the fascist salute, such was our innocence in those days of illusion. The shouts of "Viva Zorro" and "Viva Maria" rose to a crescendo as we left the quayside. Capri was on the starboard bow before the distant clamour was lost in the hum and bustle of the great and elegant ship getting into her stride for the voyage ahead.

I have described this episode in detail for, as I came to know, it was the pattern of Douglas and Mary's progress wherever they went. Even in Moscow, when Russia was enduring the pangs of rebirth, they had to have police protection and on one occasion to barricade the door of their hotel room against the multitudes who had found escape from tribulation, and consolation for their miseries, in ramshackle cinemas flickering romantic glimpses of a world as remote as heaven or on screens with projectors carried by camels that shone the comicalities of Chaplin, the acrobatics of Douglas, and the tear-raising predicaments of Mary in the dark of night over the steppes of Central Asia. In Naples, Douglas assured me, we had been lucky, for often he carried Mary on his shoulder through dangerously pressing crowds of her adorers. I would share many such mêlées with them, amazed by their equanimity until they told me that once they sought refuge in the Dolomites where they expected to be and were unrecognised. Two days incognito sufficed. Starved of acclamation, they hurried back to the civilisation that gave them in full measure its treasure and affection.

The *Roma*, outward bound, was not overpopulated. I found myself, therefore, a member of a little theatrical family, such as I had known as a boy, which kept very much to itself and passed the time in nostalgic stage gossip to which I was able to make my hereditary contribution. For, to Mary's delight, among our fellow passengers was Chauncey Olcott and his wife. Olcott had been a leading American actor-manager in whose company Mary's mother played in New York, while she, age five, was on tour with another troupe. She was still mourning the death of her actress-mother who, in hard times, had committed her, her sister Lottie, and her brother Jack to the stage so that between them they could earn enough to provide for the necessities of their transitory homes. Those early trials, when every dollar had to be fought for, earned, and frugally spent had hardened Mary's business acumen when it came to asserting her salary claims to movie magnates competing for her profit-making services. So I found that I had fallen among stage rather than film folk and that our common background would be the foundation of our lasting friendship.

Once through the Strait of Gibraltar the Atlantic was its usual unpredictable self, and, through the alternating moderate gales and brief calms, Mary kept most of the time to her cabin. Consequently, Douglas and I, enjoying hearty meals of inexhaustible variations of spaghetti and pacing our daily mile round the deck, were left much to ourselves. On the second day out he gave me his draft script of the film we were to make—a compression of Dumas's *Twenty Years After* and *The Man in the Iron Mask* into one stirring narrative. It was thirty-odd quarto pages of typescript. Six months later, for all the additions and embellishments of scriptwriters, literary advisers, and gagmen, I realised that we had exactly fulfilled his drafted intention. The noble end, when one-by-one the three musketeers and their maverick companion D'Artagnan are killed in hand-to-hand fighting with the enemies of their king, had for me no more significance than an uncompromisingly unhappy and logical ending to a heroic tale. Nor did I appreciate that for the first time Douglas would be playing a character of his own age with greying hair and with an air of authority in contrast with the reckless exuberance of his earlier D'Artagnan. Neither of us, I think, realised that in doing so he was encompassing, at what appeared to be the height of his fame and form, the death of the "fumbling boyish poet" (Alistair Cook's description). Though the actor-impresario lived on, his "personal impulse" waned when motion pictures were struck by a hurricane of sound.

Our intimate conversations, however, made increasingly clear to me the immense complexities of film as opposed to stage production, though Douglas contrived to make it seem a tremendous and exciting lark. I developed insistent qualms that, with my limited experience of even stage design, I was sailing with him under false pretences. What had I to offer in a studio staffed with artists and craftsmen expert in their several fields? One night as we made the rounds of the deck before turning in, I confessed to him my anxiety on this score and my doubts of my ability to repay his trust and kindness. He stopped and, laying his hand on my arm, said, "Laurence, if you give me one idea, your being with us will be well worthwhile." His words, akin to those of a trusty commander to his troops before battle, so bolstered my self-confidence that in the event I designed acres of sets that were the background to his last great venture—except for one involving intricate technicalities of special effects beyond my ken. The next day I drew a costume design for D'Artagnan and showed it to him when we had assembled in Mary's cabin. It pleased him well enough, but it was then he told me that he had persuaded the septuagenarian French artist, Maurice Leloir, the original illustrator of Dumas, to come to Hollywood where, as the recognised authority on the period of Louis XIV, he would design the dresses and properties and generally supervise the historical aspects of the production and the deportment of the players. The old man had been genuinely reluctant to leave Paris for the first time in his long life—but the bait of 40,000 francs and all expenses paid, including those of a nephew to escort and care for him, proved irresistible, to the film's incalculable advantage and to my own in that for months I worked in close harmony with a painter disciple of Meissonier and a scholar capable of expressing his ideas as a draughtsman with a speed and dexterity that made me feel like a laggard apprentice.

Before daybreak a week after leaving London, I was on deck watching the lights of Long Island as we steamed up the channel from Nantucket marked by gas and bell buoys. The sun rose through the mist astern; a perfect dawn would herald my immigration. I was writing letters in the saloon cabin until Douglas sent for me. I had not long to wait. I reached his side below the bridge in time to see the pinnacles of Manhattan silhouetted against the honey-coloured haze. Comparatively lowly as they were then, I was staggered by their towering array, spangled with jewels where a few of their myriad windows reflected the rising sun, their loftiness enhanced by the drab relics of old New York clustered round their feet. As we neared our berth I peered up the shadowy canyons between them where diminished men and minicars scuttled about in semitwilight. A little fleet of tugs like suckling whales nuzzled and prodded us to the landing stage where 57th Street ran into the Hudson.

While Mary, who had spent the last two days computing the dutiable value of her European purchases, fought with Irish tenacity the surprisingly discourteous customs officials (not for them the world's sweetheart but a potential dispenser of douceurs), their eyes as rapacious as those of the eagles on their insignia, Douglas charmed the reporters and photographers who, when he made me known to them, were as surprisingly friendly and polite in their curiosity in the fourth Irving to try his luck in the United States.

When Mary joined us, discomforted but defiant from the fray, she told us that the brutal officials, baffled by her computations and stung by her righteous indignation, had taken their revenge. Every piece of her baggage had been impounded and could only be recovered from the warehouse at a price. We descended the gangway to the cheers of a mob of villainous-looking cutthroats, longshoremen who gently gave way, gazing upon their returning stars with doglike devotion. I had already seen the rough and the smooth of the American way of life before I set foot on its hospitable shores.

The artists of United Artists may have been united but so were the forces of the film distributors and exhibitors who were opposed to them. The Hollywood mandarins had encouraged the circulation of the snide wisecrack that the lunatics "wanted to take charge of the asylum." D. W. Griffith, wrapped in the egocentricity of his great achievement, had no head for money; Chaplin, whose path to stardom had been the most arduous, regarded those who battened on his success with suspicion and distaste; Douglas and Mary alone were realistic and hardheaded in matters of business. Their republic of talents needed, however, a condottiere skilled in the internecine wars of film promotion, to defend their independence and to extend the frontiers of their distributing agencies and outposts of cinemas under their control.

I had little time to take in the splendours of the suite in the Waldorf Astoria—while Douglas was planning my introduction to New York and Mary exhorting her attorney on the telephone to recover her baggage without delay—before their condottiere was in our midst, filling the room with his massive and forceful presence and shattering the altruistic reverence for the art of moviemaking that had been the theme of their catechism. Joe Schenck, the president and secular strong arm of United Artists, embodied the rapacity of a robber-baron, the vitality of a basso profundo, the authority of one of Napoleon's ruder marshals, the guile of a master criminal, and the cynical good humour of a man conscious of his attributes. Nevertheless, he did not trouble to conceal his soft heart, when disengaged from confounding his competitors, which endeared him to his wife Norma Talmadge and to the many he had befriended in their hour of need. He had the physique of a Russian wrestler but was at no pains to preserve it; a drooping eyelid and twist of his lip suggested a sly arrogance that was not part of his nature. His brother, Nick, the power behind Louis B. Mayer's throne at Metro-Goldwyn-Mayer, had acquired a measure of sophisticated elegance but was the more ruthless operator. Both had been bred in the gold fields of the Yukon where their mother kept a boarding house—if I heard their friends correctly. He scrutinized me briefly, concluded I was harmless, and thereafter treated me with kindly tolerance amounting almost to the pity that snappers-up of easy money have for fools who try to earn it with their hands. Without him the consortium of artists would have succumbed to the predators of the well-established racket that had acquired the prestige of an industry.

In mounting pandemonium, as Mary's grievance became more impassioned and waiters came and went with trays of refreshments, Douglas gave Schenck a detailed summary of the company's prospects in Europe, reeling off with astonishing precision gross takings, the progress in building and buying new cinemas, and an optimistic estimate of the state of the artists' union in every country he had visited. So, what I had assumed to be a holiday, with its round of social and sporting engagements and the gracious acceptance of public homage, had in fact been the pertinent reconnaissance of an executive with a keen eye for business. I could only catch the gist of his report, for at another telephone the chairman of a bank, who had followed in Schenck's turbulent slipstream, was hectoring his broker, shouting the odds like a bookie as the stocks of an Italian bank and General Motors took a dive, and, in response to Schenck's curt asides, purchasing the declining shares as they fell ripe into his hands. Business disposed of, Mary plied me with coffee and her contempt for bureaucrats in general and customs officials in particular. Schenck regaled Douglas with ribald Hollywood gossip, collected his attendant banker, and, like Mephistopheles, vanished with a puff of smoking repartee. In ten minutes I had heard thousands of dollars change hands, huge real estate deals clinched or planned, and a vivid combat report on the fluctuating battle for the lion's share of a booming business.

That evening Douglas took me to dine with Schenck and the banker in the latter's penthouse overlooking Central Park. Thanks to Compton Mackenzie's vigorous propagation of recorded music in his journal *The Gramophone*, I had become an enthusiast for acoustic horns and fibre needles and the revelations of electric recording. The banker owned the first radiogram I had ever heard. The volume and quality of its sound amazed me—but not as much as my companions' indifference to the broken needle that distorted and destroyed each successive record of the stack it changed automatically during dinner. Later Douglas and I parted from Joe as he drove off round the Park in an open horse carriage, his straw hat tilted rakishly over one eye and his arms round the waists of two lovely girls—fresh nymphs apparently conjured by a Vaudeville Prospero from what little air there was amid the cloud-capped towers and gorgeous palaces of Manhattan.

I reached my room in the Waldorf Astoria in the early hours, exhilarated but not apparently exhausted for, as I put out my hand to turn the doorknob, blue sparks of static electricity flashed from my fingers to the brass terminal. I needed sleep, if only to convince me that I was not a dreaming somnambulist about to wake with a start the morning after I had laid aside the robes of Gaspar. Our Whitsun wiles to entice our modest audience, frugally mounted and extravagant only in the contributory gifts of the participants, were as remote in time and space as his native Florence must have seemed to Marco Polo in the pagodas of Cathay.

Stifled, I stood at the open window. I was hemmed in by glittering honeycombs framed in black screens fencing little plots of pale, protesting stars. The sun had not yet risen on my second day in the land of the free, yet I had seen the dreamy and the seamy side of motion-picture making. Whatever contribution I might be able to make, I knew that I would have a ringside seat at the unending contest between art and exploitation, fulfilling my boyhood ambition to play a part in the industry that Hollywood had made its own. I would be rooting for the artists to uphold their supremacy in the fiercely competitive show business that in the last resort depended and will forever depend on their individual powers to win the suffrage of popular audiences.

Two

Three days later I lay naked in my "drawing room," which provided the amenities of a Turkish bath, as the "Super Chief" whistled its way through scorched Kansas townships, and listlessly watched the long prairie swell roll by. At last I had leisure to sort out my own impressions of the crowded hours spent in New York and Chicago.

On Broadway we had endured a marathon performance of Eugene O'Neill's *Strange Interlude*, six hours on the stage memorable only for the curtain line of the first lap—"My men!"—uttered by Lynn Fontanne with feline satisfaction as she sat between the slaves of her sexual lamp. New York playgoers liked to boast of their own original performance of unprecedented fortitude in the cause of culture, though most of them, I dare say, found, as I did, the play tediously pretentious and much of it incomprehensible. Hurrying from one extreme of show business to another, after a folksy breakfast at one of Child's restaurants punctuated by greetings from friends and fans, Douglas introduced me to two experiments in film production and exhibition that, though he was not aware of it, foreshadowed the end of the age of movie innocence he knew to be golden and believed to be lasting. For on our way to visit Mr. Roxy, the builder and proprietor of the largest cinema in the world, we visited the vaults of the Chase National Bank, where in a steel drawer lay the tangible tenets of his faith—two million dollars in state bonds which he had put aside for the rainy day as yet unpresaged by any clouds on the horizon of his optimism. In the sumptuous office of the Roxy Theatre, I was moved to pity for the pale, haggard, chain-smoking tycoon evidently suffering from coronary destruction caused by the Frankenstein picture house he had created. The secret of the exhibitor's success was, he told Douglas, the provision of extravagant and meaty stage shows sandwiched between films to offset their lack of drawing power at the box office. With tired pride he took us to the back of the grand circle. Remote in a vast and chilling cavern, on a screen that seemed no larger than a pocket handkerchief, a film flickered away its tenuous hold on an audience immune to the subtle contrivances of its makers to stir emotions. Then, up went the lights, a full orchestra went into blaring action, and the curtains parted to reveal a pantomime of gorgeous vulgarity featuring the beauty chorus known to the New World, thanks to Mr. Roxy's indefatigable promotion, as the "Rockettes." I could sense Douglas's deep distaste for exploitation of this kind.

From that super cinema we went to a small private projection room off Broadway. There we saw a gangster film remarkable only for its electronic accompaniment of music and audible pistol shots and jaw punches, with spasms of dialogue that sounded like Feodor Chaliapin singing under water. We agreed that if a film such as we were about to make could be issued with a recorded score it could be shown in cinemas large and small with the effect Griffith had given to *The Birth of a Nation* by employing orchestras to tour with the film. It now seems incredible that Douglas did not hear in this cacophonic experiment in sound-film the knell of his own career. Perhaps he did, but kept his counsel.

In Chicago, to fill the six-hour hiatus between trains, we drove to a suburban golf course to join Bobby Jones on his round in an international golf match. Douglas loved champions of any kind. In his company I would soon become familiar with the world's aces and would recognise in most of them the modest self-assurance and good humour of that elegant and easygoing golfer. As an athlete, Douglas could have matched most of them in any sport. For his last film, *The Gaucho*, he sought not the instruction but the example of an expert stockwhipper from Australia—to such purpose that, as I can testify, his young assistants would, without a qualm, let him flick the ash off the cigarettes between their lips with a crack of the twenty-foot lash. By closely observing the action of any such exponent, he could analyse its rhythm and balance and in a very short time imitate it to perfection.

When we boarded "The Indian Chief," the platform was thronged with reporters, photographers, and film fans swarming on their queen, Mary Pickford. These Chicagoans were the first to hear and to see that her fabulous curls had fallen to the scissors of a New York hairdresser and to learn, not without dismay, that the world's sweetheart had put her hair up. If the Pope had appeared in St. Peter's with a full-bottomed wig, his global flock would have been no less shocked. The crowd did not temper their curiosity as to the shorn lamb who dodged their speculations on her future with an inscrutable smile. Douglas, himself uncertain as to what her impulsive haircut portended, skillfully parried the imposition of importunate columnists. But Mary's pretty head, regardless of her coiffure, was well screwed on. As it turned out, she was a jump ahead of him and her fellow stars as our super-train, hooting like a wistful owl, began its 3000-mile haul westward. Now our party occupied the whole of one coach.

For the first two days and nights, I sweated it out in my luxurious oven, its walls hot to the touch, its unconditioned air murdering sleep. So, on the third, I welcomed Douglas's call shortly before dawn to take me to the observation car to view the foothills of the Rockies. Though their distant peaks were curtained with cloud, they were a welcome landfall after the oceanic horizons of the featureless plains. Nearing Albuquerque, while I breakfasted, I watched a wedding procession shuffling down the street of a forlorn Indian village towards a parched adobe church—a priest and his acolytes in sun-bleached vestments, the bride and bridegroom in their western Sunday best, a few dishevelled redskin guests, and behind them two feathered braves letting off guns to keep the evil spirits at bay. The happy pair were having the best of both metaphysical worlds.

Like Hansel and Gretel, I left postcard traces of my journey at every stop lest I became lost to my distant family. From Needles, California, on the desert's frontier, I wrote (with the rhythms of Masefield still lingering in my dizzy head):

Along the trail to Santa Fe
The bleaching bones of oxen lay
Of pioneers who led the way
Now by the smooth and metalled track,
Battered, absurd, a rusty black
A gutted Ford lies on its back
To mark our going.

Along the road to Santa Fe
The lean and hungry beasts of prey
Prowl round a stranded Chevrolet
Forlorn and puzzled;
Imagine how these creatures feel
On finding, when they seek a meal,
Unappetizing bits of steel
Where once they guzzled.

Praise God from whom all blessings flow
From Kansas to New Mexico
The motorists in thousands go
Making their Westing
Beneath the tail, the pioneers
Unchanging with the changing years
The roar of traffic in their ears
Lie quietly resting

At Pasadena Station a horde of liege men and women and loyal subjects welcomed their king and queen safely returned from a crusade to win the hearts of Europeans to the idolatry on which the inhabitants of its

Ephesus—thousands of suntanned players, writers, craftsmen, technicians, and executors—depended for their fairy affluence. Douglas
handed me over to his eighteen-year-old son, "Junior." As the crown
prince of Hollywood, to whom Jack Barrymore had played the dual
roles of Pointz and Falstaff, he had a sophisticated poise beyond his
years. He had, of course, hereditary right of entry into the film studios
and had already made the most of it. Later, his performance as a Royal
Flying Corps pilot at the Western Front in one of the first films on the
subject, *The Dawn Patrol,* was, as I was qualified to judge, remarkably
authentic. Not content, however, to exercise his hereditary privilege, he
was soon to play *Young Woodley* in Hollywood's live theatre and to win
the praise of sceptical critics. Barrymore was the perfect, if raffish, tutor
to a young actor of many talents in a cultural desert, for, as the sovereign of the royal family of the American stage, his erratic genius was
harnessed, like that of his sister Ethel, to sound traditional techniques.
Though he was then working at the United Artists Studios, Barrymore
was not there to meet us. A night or two earlier he had been knocked
out in a brawl at the Biltmore Hotel and carried home unconscious.
Forty years before he had been the friend of my Uncle Laurence, who
had been briefly betrothed to Ethel and in 1914 was tragically drowned
in a shipping disaster. Earlier, as a boy, his romantic spirit had been
stirred by Maurice Leloir's superb illustrations to Dumas's *The Three
Musketeers.* When semiconscious on the morning after his fracas he
asked his valet for a newspaper, he could barely focus on the headlines,
but enough to read: FAIRBANKS BRINGS MAURICE LELOIR AND
LAURENCE IRVING TO HOLLYWOOD. Convinced that he, too, was
now dead, he groaned a curse, turned his face to the wall, and relapsed
into oblivion.

At the wheel of a powerful two-seater coupé, Junior, with an engaging
detachment, concluded an informative and wryly humorous prologue to
the motion-picture pageant in which I was to play a minor role. Of that
drive I remember only the succession of gigantic roadside advertisements
in dazzling white frames that made me feel as though I were being
whisked through an exhibition of pictures painted by a prolific artist of
impressive vulgarity. Never having visited Spain or Italy, the Mediterranean houses and pseudo-estancias struck me as original and picturesque and complementary to the brown, arid hills on which they were artfully perched by real estate dealers. All too soon we turned off Hollywood
Boulevard, down a street overshadowed by a wall of buildings, and drove
through steel gates, guarded apparently by a Texan philosopher and his
Alsatian dog, into an enclave where soon I would have to justify the fabulous expense of my transportation thither.

In its centre stood three studios and the carpenter's shop, each like an outsize airplane hangar. On two sides these structures were enclosed by buildings that met at right angles made by Douglas's and Mary's head-quarters, their purposes and uses contrary for all their contiguity. Douglas's dressing room, in effect a hall with an ever open door, led to a steam bath and a cold plunge. To Douglas, privacy was a deprivation. At all hours members of his court and visitors were welcome—at their own risk. For beside his dressing room table was an armchair into which the un-wary, conscious of the privilege of his warm invitation to take a seat, sank in prospect of an intimate chat with their distinguished host, only to leap from it with a yelp of dismay as their posteriors tingled from an electric shock galvanised by a switch concealed under his dressing table. This hospitable snare, eagerly anticipated and relished by an audience de-lighting in practical jokes of any kind, betrayed, perhaps, his Teutonic an-cestry, akin to the ponderous pranks played by Edward VII on his long-suffering courtiers.

In contrast Mary's bungalow had the cloistered calm of a nunnery where its Mother Superior welcomed only faithful friends and business associ-ates in awe of her perspicacity. There Mary, when not herself filming, spun daily from the threads of her talent as an artist and femme d'affaires the web of financial security for herself and her dependant relatives. Having been the family breadwinner since she was five years old, industry and thrift had become as obsessive to her as her faith in Christian Science. Later she and Douglas took me to see Karel and Josef Capek's *Insect Play* at the Biltmore Theatre. In it appears the Beetle forever rolling a snowball pile of treasured rubbish. Thereafter, I nicknamed her the "Beetle" which, with her Irish sense of the ridiculous, she accepted as a term of endearment. Since then the all too intermittent correspondence from her, which have af-firmed our life-long affection for each other, have born this entomophilous signature.

Beyond the studios was a vast open space, "the lot," which from a dis-tance appeared to be the relics of a world fair exhibiting every style and period of architecture known to man—a jumble of facades of stone, mar-ble tiles, and brick skillfully rendered in plaster on frameworks of timber and chicken wire. There were the recognisable backgrounds of long-remembered films preserved intact by the perpetual sunshine until they outlived useful adaptation and were demolished to make room for new productions. Though more substantial than stage settings, each was trun-cated to the limits of the camera's lines of sight, their jagged silhouettes reminding me of a shell-torn Belgian town. Tucked away in a corner were the hutments and horse-lines of a squadron of Polish cavalry—exiles who had transferred their allegiance to a make-believe state, ever ready to go into action as mounted cowboys, Indians, uhlans, musketeers, or U.S. troopers, as films demanded. In proud isolation the officers and soldiers maintained the dignity and disciplines of their old order amidst an egalitarian society that could neither appreciate nor honour the military values that had enabled them to fight their way out of the bloody disintegration of Eastern Europe.

That first day in a film studio was spent in a whirlwind of introductions that stripped me of all memories but one—my presentation (for such in its regality it seemed) to David Wark Griffith who, in my esteem, had towered above his fellow United Artists. He was of smaller stature than I expected but his features were, like my grandfather's, those that would have distinguished a leader of any profession. He received me with polite gravity and accepted my homage as though it was his due. I was shocked to find this pioneer, whose inventive genius and passionate faith in the new medium had been the impetus on which the whole rickety edifice of Hollywood was based, was so little respected by the mandarins of the dynasty he had founded. Every foot of film threaded through the gates of its hundreds of cameras every day bore the imprint of his daring experiments. Every reel in its can bore witness to the emotional impact on audiences of the rhythmic cutting and selective apposition of close, medium, and long shots from which he had created a new language, a visual Esperanto that parrot producers had long since taken for granted as their native tongue. When the cognoscenti belatedly condescended to recognise motion pictures as an "art form," they taught their disciples to genuflect not to Griffith, but to Sergei Eisenstein and Vsevolod Pudovkin, whose technical mastery was derived entirely from him. It was somehow more comfortable to orient the cult of film appreciation on Russians committed to an ideology than on an American whose concern for human values was too generous to be confined to any political doctrine. So I found myself face to face with a dispirited visionary accepting his loss of aesthetic and financial independence and fulfilling his obligations to the corporation by remaking an early potboiler, *The Battle of the Sexes,* which he did not bother to endorse with his signature. Though I met him again, I was unable to unwind the bandages of his wounded egotism.

He had learned the bitter lesson that sooner or later any director of film or stage productions has to face—namely, that the public will only acclaim the players who directly stir their emotions. Film and play goers are unconcerned with the auxiliary talents that contribute to a performance which they and the performers together make a unique experience. That is why the players, in the long run, regained the authority that at the time was denied them. Whenever I am made aware of the desperate efforts of theatrical organisations to prevent the emergence of actors or actresses as leaders of their profession, I think of my encounter with the mighty but fallen Griffith who drove his protégés to stardom denying them only the public credit that, rightly or wrongly, he deemed his sole right. In the end the public had its way, exalted his players above him, and became blind to his name in lights on the canopies of cinemas it could no longer fill. Now, like the student of Prague, he could not see the reflection of the proud master he had been. Nevertheless, it was honourable and just that Fairbanks, Pickford, and Chaplin acknowledged his preeminence by making him, though his force was spent, their ally in united resistance to the dominance of their art by shabby entrepreneurs.

Douglas and Mary invited me to stay with them at Pickfair until Maurice Leloir and Leon Barry arrived from France when, perhaps, the three of us could live together in one of the pseudo-Spanish apartment houses on an estate known as Andalusia. When at the end of that long day we took our lighthearted departure from the studio, dusk was falling and with it the carefree spirits of my hosts. I was surprised to see that the family Rolls Royce was preceded and followed by less elegant vehicles full of armed guards; this was a necessary precaution, it was explained to me with some embarrassment, against gangsters who had threatened to kidnap Mary and hold her for ransom. A few hours later I was gazing from my bedroom window on the moonlit garden. A man was lurking in the shadows of the surrounding trees. Accidentally I brushed against the lavatory seat, which fell with a resounding clang on its pan. The man whipped round and, as quick on the draw as William S. Hart, weaved his revolver to and fro, ready to riddle the imagined intruder. Relieved to know he was a guard and not a bandit, I crept back to bed ashamed of having triggered off a false alarm but deeply impressed by the protection of the peacefully sleeping household. This was not the last time that the sinister undercurrent below the serene surface of Hollywood's public image intruded on, what Douglas so vehemently insisted, was the best of all possible worlds. In a way, I was glad to know that the West was still a bit wild.

Pickfair was an unpretentious house of no particular style, though certainly more English than Spanish—the sort of house a prosperous Edwardian actor-manager might have built on the river above Maidenhead. The interior decorator had evidently intended to furnish it in hotel-Adam style, but, thanks to Douglas and Mary's liking for homely comfort, the rigours of the period had been alleviated. The big sitting room, open to the hall, had a large well-upholstered settee and deep armchairs. After dinner these were arranged to face the far wall, where a discreetly hidden screen was lowered on which the latest motion pictures were projected from a booth concealed in the staircase. To watch these while my hosts made running commentaries on them and on occasion, for the screen reached the floor, the substantial Chaplin joined the shadowy performers to make uproarious and well-deserved fun of the banalities of directors and players, was an education in the pitfalls of making motion pictures, which all too easily could lapse into bathos.

If Pickfair was Hollywood's Palais Royale and the mecca of distinguished visitors or ambitious film folk, its sovereigns' court was remarkable for its modesty and constancy. Douglas spent his brief weekends with a trinity of old cronies—Kenneth Davenport, Earl Brown, and Tom Geraghty. The first two were companions of his Broadway theatrical youth and the third an Irish newspaperman turned scriptwriter, with the double-barrelled wit of his twin nationality and flair for contriving the kind of practical jokes in which Douglas and Chaplin delighted. Many years before, the impecunious young Douglas, leaving for a midwinter tour of the Midwest, had accepted the loan of his friend Kenneth's only overcoat. Later, when his benefactor developed tuberculosis, Douglas believed he had sacrificed his health for him and thereafter saw to it that he was never in need of a livelihood or the best medical attention. Kenneth was a quiet American of great charm and made me his companion in evening forays for entertainment. Earl Brown I recognised as an actor such as I had known in my father's company, Irish but equable and with the dignified deportment of a professional, ready to play Leontes, Laertes, or Lancelot Gobbo at the drop of the appropriate cue. I count my acceptance as the fourth of this congenial entourage the most acceptable honour I have ever received.

Though this court, when occasion rose, could be decorous enough and observe a sort of easy going protocol (though ever at risk of its being undermined by the incorrigible Chaplin), the hilarious informality of its weekend sessions was more akin to that of King Cole than of St. James. Mary was a diligent and thrifty housewife, but she found it difficult to count the linens when she might be called at any minute to applaud an impromptu charade for her diversion. Apart from her attractive nieces, no other ladies-in-waiting from the principality, where the beauty of its women was almost monotonous, had been admitted to these frolics. But at the time of my appointment, Junior was ardently courting an up-and-coming film actress, Joan Crawford, who soon found herself in this genial company. The Texan peasant, as it were, beloved by the handsome prince had gained her footing in the studios by the unflagging exercise of her powerful personality in a milieu where even such beauty as hers was commonplace. In her continuing struggle for recognition she had little time to cultivate the domestic arts. Eager to win Mary's approval as a step-daughter-in-law, she brought to those Sunday gatherings a piece of needlework and, during lulls in our follies, stitched away demurely. As the weeks went by, her stitching seemed to make little progress so I suspected that, like Penelope, she unravelled this effective property to make it last through the run of her betrothal. Douglas, though at this stage he did not betray it, must have had misgivings at the prospect of a grand paternity incompatible with the youth and agility of his heroic impersonations.

Chaplin was often the master of our revels. His caprices might foreshadow sequences in later masterpieces. One, I remember, was pregnant with apocalyptic prophesy. The recent Treaty of Locarno appeared to have buried the Franco-German hatchet; the world seemed assured of the peaceful pursuit of its occupation. Hitler was still a small-time politician. Yet, one afternoon, Chaplin emerged from the backdrop house wearing one of Mary's chemises, which reached to the sock suspenders above his cloth-topped boots, on his head a German *pickelhaube,* and in his hands a large globe (an ornament from Douglas's soi-disant "study"), and on the sunlit lawn he rehearsed the balletic dance of the dictator, with which, ten years later with brave and cocky impertinence, he alone would make public ridicule of the führer when he had the craven world in thrall.

I first set eyes on Chaplin literally in the flesh when we met in Douglas's steam bath. I introduced myself. Perhaps the honour in which he, as a boy actor in London, held my grandfather (he had attended his funeral in Westminster Abbey) commended me to him. This was another rich legacy I inherited from "the antique," for the objects of Charlie's reverence were few. The setting of our first meeting might have come from a play by George Bernard Shaw. Through clouds of vapour and in the infernal heat, he looked what he was—an imp in the train of Mephistopheles working subversively on the side of the angels. I soon found that we had more frivolous bonds and lively prejudices in common—the basis of an enduring friendship. He had scarcely begun to tell me of his recent visit to William Randolph Hearst's monumental folly in the hills of San Simeon than we were joined by Sam Goldwyn who, wrapped in a towel and with the nutcracker features of one of Leonardo's grotesques, might have been a subsidiary character from Raphael's *School of Athens.*

Not long before, Goldwyn had insinuated himself, sponsored no doubt by Joe Schenck, into the bosom of the United Artists. This was no mean achievement, for earlier in her career Mary had taught him an overdue lesson in good manners. Douglas and Charlie were by nature antipathetic to the hierarchy of the industry he represented. In fact, Goldwyn had done much to raise the level of its products. His flair for detecting and assembling talents resulted in some of the most entertaining and distinguished films of that period. His promotion was instinctive, for he had no cultural pretensions; his malapropisms (though they were often used as pegs for others to hang their wit on) are legendary. For all this I, and apparently his associates, did not find him agreeable company. He did not disguise a resentful arrogance towards the artists on whom his self-expression depended. Years later, a Jewish producer, for whom I had a great affection, explained to me the compulsive attraction that filmmaking had for men of his faith. The commandments that expressly forbad the making of graven images precluded them from practising the sculptural or graphic arts. Many found an outlet in music, particularly as virtuoso instrumentalists. But the theatre, and then films, provided an irresistible opportunity to manipulate an art that was not representational within the meaning of Mosaic law. Until recently, the theatricals had resisted their participation. The players, masters of their playhouses, had no wish to share their hard-won profits with anyone. A few, like the Frohmans, had gained authority over the stage and had used it with admirable discretion. Then came moving pictures, with all the chance they afforded for cool gambling, ruthless exploitation, the glamorous power of exalting amorphous golden calves for the world to worship plus the provision of undreamed of percentages. In no time they gained control of the burgeoning industry. And by this time in Hollywood, they reigned supreme and could afford to regard with tolerant amusement the handful of artists who had thrown off their yoke and might live to regret it. Goldwyn had been among the first in the field, and his name will survive as a progenitor of Metro-Goldwyn-Mayer. But by inclination he was a maverick producer. Once admitted to United Artists he could enjoy total independence.

Chattering away to Charlie, I was unaware of Goldwyn's eminence or of the mischief afoot for his discomfiture. Word had got around that, though such excessive ablutions were not to his taste, he suspected that in the steam bath business confidences were exchanged in the sweat of his colleagues' brows and that, in his own interest, he should join the perspiring elite. This particular intrusion of commerce into what might be called a boiling of friends was not to be endured. Suddenly the light went out, the steam was turned full on, and the stygian suffocating darkness was rent with three tremendous explosions that set my eardrums ringing. When the lights went up, Goldwyn had vanished. Charlie, smiling inscrutably, seemed unperturbed. He had been, of course, party to the plot; his hand was on the steam valve, and one of Douglas's trainers had switched off the lights while another fired three blank cartridges from a revolver. Goldwyn rarely returned. The baths were safe for "thermocracy."

Even the pen of Aldous Huxley flowing with mordant ink had failed to evoke the fantastic banalities of the press tycoon William Randolph Hearst, as he entertained guests and sycophants at his huge home in California. Chaplin's Rabelaisian account, when we resumed our conversation, of his philistine night entertainments in that ill-assorted fastness of palaces and churches wrenched from their European foundations and reassembled in the arid hills of San Simeon. No doubt the yarns he spun of this coterie made the most of its depravities and of the irresistible exercise of power and corruption by its saturnine Lord of Misrule. I came to wonder how he could play the court jester to a ruthless plutocrat who seemed all that was alien to

Chaplin's political sentiments and convictions. Hearst was the embodiment of those forces and pretensions that were the target of his ridicule. This flaw in Chaplin's philosophy was later revealed in his frank and very moving autobiography. I felt, then, that at best he was wasting his time in such company; at worst, it may have given him the illusion of having friends in the corrupt courts of California. When, in fact, he had need of them, they were conspicuous in their absence. It would be idle to deny that I was vastly amused by his performance for my benefit. The company had been enlivened by the presence of Elinor Glyn to whom the elect of Los Angeles deferred as a reliable mistress in the study of English etiquette. These revelations, however, inhibited me from seeking an invitation to this depressing Babylon. Douglas and Mary, being neither in fear of Hearst's displeasure or in need of the imagined power of his press, treated him with polite reserve. They were occasionally his hosts but never his guests and warned me not to be drawn into that galère. The palace Hearst had built for his adored Marion Davies on the shore of the Pacific at Santa Monica was next door to the Fairbanks's own bungalow. Douglas took me there on the occasion when Jimmy Walker, the mountebank mayor of New York, was soliciting Hearst's support for Al Smith, the presidential candidate opposing Herbert Hoover. Only two years before, Walker had been the target of vituperative attacks by the Hearst newspapers when he stood for election against John Francis Hylan, who would have been a pliant tool in the hands of their proprietor with an eye to the White House. Defiantly putting the power of the press to the test, Walker easily defeated his opponent. Now all was forgiven if not forgotten. Only the previous night I had seen the mayor of the world's largest city do a song and soft-shoe dance with Claudette Colbert in the interval before the premiere of her latest film. The audience of film executors and stars were evidently delighted. I tried to imagine the reaction of Londoners to a similar performance by their Lord Mayor at the Hippodrome. But I was conscious of Douglas and Mary's embarrassment that I should witness such antics so incompatible with the dignity of office.

Hearst's appearance and manner were all that Chaplin had led me to expect. Tall, heavily built with shambling gait and a damp flabby handshake, his expressionless mask was that of an ascetic and possible benevolent scholar. But his pale grey eyes had the pitiless stare of a goat and his lips were mercilessly thin. His high-pitched, petulant voice suggested that a soundtrack had been synchronised to the wrong image. He conducted me through rooms papered, as it were, with old masters, though, as he commented on them sotto voce, even I could see that most of them were palpable fakes. His personality was neither hypnotic nor despotic. I assumed that he derived the power he exulted in from the wealth he inherited and the media of self-assertion he had acquired. I was at a loss to understand the awe in which this flaccid ogre was held, as I knew, by British diplomats and statesmen. That many of Charlie Evans's novelists spoke of him with reverence was natural enough, for his glossy magazines paid princely fees for their contributions.

I was soon made aware of another paradox in the weird society that exalted him. His harpy columnists in the Los Angeles and San Francisco *Examiner* were muckrakers with a vengeance. Most of that vulnerable film colony lived in eager hope of their puffs or in deadly fear of their reckless innuendos. Female gossip writers seemed to lead a charmed life, immune to actions for libel which, in England, would have ended their careers at the Old Bailey. Here they thrived on calumny and capricious favouritism, secure under their proprietor's protection. His power, I gathered, was such that, in 1924, he had been able to suppress all references in his own and other newspapers to an incident that was and to this day remains a mystery.

On November 11th, Hearst and his mistress, Marion Davies, embarked in his yacht *Oneida* from San Pedro with about a dozen guests including Chaplin, the novelist Elinor Glyn, his gossip harpy Louella Parsons, and Thomas Ince. Ince was a distinguished film director, second only to D. W. Griffith as a master of his craft. At the time, Hearst was hoping to persuade him to direct the next film he was producing and so to promote the career of Marion Davies as a movie star. A day or two later the yacht berthed at San Diego. Ince was seen being carried ashore, appearing to have suffered head wounds. He was rushed to his home in Hollywood where a few hours later he died. Two days later his body was cremated. A doctor had certified his death from heart failure. No inquest was held to establish the cause of his death, and the district attorney of Los Angeles affirmed that there was no evidence of foul play.

Bill Menzies had confided to me these facts and rumours that all of Ince's fellow guests had been sworn to secrecy. My criminological education by my father inspired me to discover more about so strange an affair. Though Douglas, Mary, and Chaplin had attended Ince's funeral, they did not respond to my interrogation. That several less discreet informants expected me to believe that their assertions were credible implied that life was still relatively cheap in Roaring Camp. I had yet to learn that in any event death was not a subject for polite conversation in that earthly paradise.

So I was left only to conclude that, if a man in Hearst's position could be so bemused by *folie de grandeur* as to imagine that, if the press and the police could be effectively silenced, his success in doing so would lead to suspicions that he had something sinister to conceal and the wildest conjectures as to its nature, he had only himself to blame for the popular assumption that his motives were criminal.

My curiosity already had been excited by a most bizarre aspect of life, or rather of death, in California. Eddie Knoblock had described to me the macabre commercialism of American undertakers—morticians, as they styled themselves—and of their keen competition in the art of embalming. He had attended the lying-in-state of Rudolph Valentino—lost all too soon for millions of his infatuated admirers and still annually celebrated by his mourners in the memorial column of *The Times*. As Knoblock passed by the open casket, a little man in black sidled up to him and murmured: "How do you like *our* smile?" He told me, too, of the trade magazine *The Morticians Journal* and of its grotesque mortuary advertisements.

A CASKET ON SUNNY SIDE
DON'T LET THE HOT WEATHER GET AT YOU
USE NECRODENT FOR THE DEAR DEAD TEETH

Thirty years later Evelyn Waugh would make bitter game of these elaborate obsequies and the commercial exploitation of bereavement—natural, perhaps, in a materialistic society that, unlike the rest of the western world, had not had to shovel the remains of millions of its young men without ceremony under the earth where they had fallen. Douglas, when he saw a copy of *The Morticians Journal* on my table, was shocked by my mockery of it. I was chastened but not persuaded that there was any mortal alternative between the crematorium and Madame Tussaud's.

When Maurice Leloir and Leon Barry arrived, we set up our ménage in Andalusia. We shared a large sitting room and the services of a matronly Madame Vinard, though no Trilby was forthcoming to be our model *mascotte*. Leloir appeared to be frail for the change in environment and strenuous work that lay ahead of us. Noting his bow legs and that he was evidently no horseman, I attributed them, thanks to my early indoctrination in infant maladies, to rickets. My diagnosis was confirmed when he told me that, during the commune of 1871, as he lay, a weakened emaciated youth, in his garret room in Paris, a communist press-gang searching for recruits to man the barricades took one look at the recumbent skeletal figure, decided he was dead, pulled the sheet over his face, and left him in peace. Yet his strong white hair *en brosse* should have told me that his frailty was deceptive, for mentally and physically he proved to be as alert and vigorous as the best of us.

As an art student he was inspired, not by the grandiose works of Ingres and Delacroix, but by the genre painter, Meissonier, an able exponent of the deliberate style of the Dutch school then at the height of his popularity; his detailed evocations of France's military glory under Napoleon Bonaparte had ready sales. He was a masterly draughtsman, and his disciples, such as Bonchot and Leloir, excelled as illustrators exploiting aquarelle as a medium with arresting virtuosity. Like their fellow painters in Victorian England, they were well served by accomplished steel engravers, who reproduced their drawings with a tonal and effectual truth matched by Doré with his direct process of soft ground etchings by his own hand.

Leloir spoke only his native tongue, but so slowly and with such simplicity of phrase that, helped out by Barry's workaday stage-English, my halting French did not hinder our mutual understanding. He was an uncompromising Parisian, making no concessions during his first absence from his beloved city. He crossed the Atlantic in *La France,* and in Hollywood patronised only one restaurant known as Musso Frank's, which had some resemblance to French cuisine. I could not have had two more charming, courteous, and good-humoured companions to live with in such close intimacy for our long spell of exile. There was, however, a cuckoo in our nest who, at the outset, disastrously jeopardised our good relations with our American hosts.

With Douglas's approval and at his expense, Leloir had brought with him a nephew to assure that he had the care and attention necessary for such an adventure. Both Barry and I were a trifle confused when the old man alluded to his companion as *"mon fils."* Was this gangling youth, Max, the issue of an earlier romantic indiscretion? Leloir was well able to look after himself; indeed, it seemed as though he was nursemaid to his offspring when every morning I heard him rap on the door of Max's bedroom and shout *"Sept heure et demi!"* to rouse his sluggard attendant.

Living with Max was like acting in a film with Fernandel. He was tall and gangling, radiating simple-minded innocence; dressed, as was his habit, in white from head to toe and crowned with a straw boater, he was perfectly cast as *"le rosier de Madame Husson"*; his reaction to Hollywood was that of a Muslim entering paradise. Soon he was distracted from the care of his uncle by the ravishing beauties eager to serve him in shops and restaurants and particularly by those, who as extras or bit players, thronged our studio.

As his uncle's protégé he had the run of the United Artists lot, though he had no need to run, for on every hand were irresistible invitations to dalliance. "Pree-ty gels!" he would confide to me, rolling his eyes and baring his equine teeth in a satyric grin, after an exhausting day of temptation in the magic gardens. To the girls he seemed cute, and their native kindness entranced him as that of the Huaheine Island, Tahiti enraptured the crew of the *Bounty.* They were, however, less naive than their Polynesian sisters. Thus, his days were spent stalking enchantresses dexterous at critical disengagement.

While my own designs were taking shape, nearby a magnificent replica of a Carpathian market town had been completed where shooting of a war epic directed for Sam Goldwyn by Sam Taylor was well advanced. The close action shots had been taken prior to the spectacular climax of the film, when the town would be demolished by shellfire. For that scene, hundreds of extras had been engaged to provide crowds of peasants and regiments of Austrian and Russian infantry; Hollywood had been combed for Slavic beauties to lend glamour to the holocaust.

At H-Hour I was, by invitation, at the director's side. The atmosphere was tense. Weeks of planning were to be put to the test. The groups of extras were marshalled at their starting points. Cameramen were making last-minute tests, dipping exposed film into their portable developing tanks. The demolitionists were overhauling detonators, fuses, and electric circuits. The baroque fountain that stood out against the shadowy colonnade of the town hall beyond it gushed water. One by one, assistant directors reported that all was correct and ready, while others, through their megaphones, called for silence. They got it, the authentic prebombardment hush. Sam disengaged a well-chewed cigar from his teeth and with this baton set his orchestra in motion. A dozen hand-cranked cameras whirred a pianissimo introduction.

The percussion entered with a vengeance. Deafening explosions created clouds of smoke flushed here and there with flames. The fountain flew apart and spouted chunks of masonry. Buildings collapsed and spirituous fire consumed the wreckage. Smoke eclipsed the Californian sun. A sulphurous curtain hid the set from view. The extras were held on leash until it began to clear.

Then through a rift, a beam of sunlight lit up the ruins of the town hall. A susurration of horror rose from the crowd intent upon the scene. There in the centre arch of the shattered colonnade, illuminated like an archangel immaculately white against a black void, stood Max, dazed, perhaps, but grinning courageously as though to reassure us that he was unscathed.

As the murk cleared, the ruin of the long-planned effect was apparent. The extras, always loyal to any production they served, became an angry mob and menacingly advanced upon Max, still blissfully unaware of the enormity of his intrusion. Assistant directors rushed to head off the avengers and hustled their intended victim out of sight. Sam sank into his chair. His bowed head concealed his emotion; as a director of Harold Lloyd's comedies, the humour of this denouement had not escaped him.

When the news reached old Leloir, he was distraught. The magnitude of the calamity he understood—but not the cost of it, for he immediately offered to recompense the producers. Not all the half-million francs that had lured him from Paris would suffice. The courteous rejection of his offer only deepened his shame. That evening, we, in our little foreign enclave, were much dispirited. But, in Hollywood, memories and fame are short lived. Max's infamy was soon forgotten; discreetly he sought other and happier hunting grounds.

Such was the background to my working days and indeed to my waking hours, for soon I was totally committed to rekindling the splendour of

Le Roi Soleil and to furnishing the daily adventures and misadventures of D'Artagnan and the Three Musketeers. Only those who have given months of their lives to making a motion picture can understand this prolonged absorption in a task that, however frivolous and ephemeral it may seem to wiseacres, depends for its success on the loyal and attentive co-operation of the humblest member of the unit engaged on it. The fact that Douglas was reinvesting a million of the dollars he had earned as an actor-producer in the art he served was, to one of my ancestry and upbringing, an imperative challenge to do the best I could for him.

THREE

As a rule, work on the lot was in full swing by eight o'clock in the morning. I had been given a pleasant studio on the first floor of a building, between the main gate and Douglas's barn-like gymnasium; beneath it was the projection room where we assembled at noon to see the rushes—prints of the previous day's work. During those first weeks I was at my drawing board until 6:00 in the evening, with an interval for lunch usually in the senior executives' restaurant. At first I was subject to a good deal of banter from our director Allan Dwan, who was suspicious of "limey" aesthetes. I was no match for the lightning wisecrack, for I was one of those frustrated verbal duelists with a feeble guard under attack who, hours later in bed, thinks up a devastating riposte that would have silenced my antagonist. One day, when I was beginning to find my feet in this strange but stimulating arena, Dwan, with a knowing wink at his companion and a nod in my direction, began "Did you ever hear the story of the English man who arrived in Boston?"

Like a subtitle there flashed upon the screen of my mind: "That's how Boston began, wasn't it?"

This inspired repartee delighted the picadors and even the matador was in the future more cautious in baiting such an unpredictable bull.

I had been immediately taken in hand by Robert Fairbanks. He was shorter than his brother, nut brown from his engineering days in Colorado, and had black penetrating eyes and a crumpled weather-beaten visage that reminded me of portraits of Cortés's fellow-conquistadors. His quiet sardonic humour made plain, as our intimacy grew, that he had no illusions as to Douglas's character and foibles. His mission in life was to humour him without curbing his infectious enthusiasm, which was the source of all their fortunes. At the outset he made me understand the significance of their independence amid the welter of the reckless extravagance and power-politics that prevailed in other studios and the necessity for intelligent economy which could best be effected by hard work and a sense of responsibility. Rarely a day passed that was not enlivened by some fantastic Douglas idea which had to be explored in detail. While Robert kept a tight hand on expenditures, he managed to do so with such tact that no whim of Douglas ever appeared rejected, but, if too fanciful, it would be subtly shelved ostensibly at his own suggestion.

I realised I had to overcome Robert's justifiable scepticism of the tyros that Douglas imported from Europe. My predecessor had been the poet Robert Nichols. My slight acquaintance of him made me wonder how his turbulent, melancholy, and rhapsodic spirit had been tamed into effective cooperation. In fact, his eccentricity had become a legend. All remembered him with affection as a stranger from outer space, and even Robert was reconciled to having such an entertaining and provocative guest on his payroll.

I could not have wished for a wiser mentor or more knowledgeable instructor in the complex technicalities that I had to master before I began interpreting Douglas's scenic dreams on paper. Over one or two dinners with his friendly family in a rather dark but cosy house in Laurel Canyon, he taught me the basic principles of camera angles and the focal length of various lenses. I soon discovered that I was blessed with 35mm vision—that is to say that whatever I composed on paper of 3×4 dimensions would be accepted by such a lens and transmitted more or less accurately to the negative. This fortuitous optical aptitude gave me great confidence when I came to design settings at accelerating speed.

Before it is too late, I feel it may be worth recording the reactions of a novitiate to the conception, preparation, construction, and filming of the first and, as it turned out, the largest set of the many I built in the course of the next months. For all that were to follow were in their execution repetitious of this first.

The action of *The Man in the Iron Mask* was for the most part laid in the environs of the Palace St. Germain-en-Laye. Fortunately, all trace of the building had vanished long ago so I was free to rely entirely on my imagination within the framework of the period. My first obligation was to provide a convincing and picturesque background for the stately and combative sequences that Douglas envisaged for a film as grandiose in conception as it was brisk in action. When the last shot was in the can, I had, apparently, fulfilled my job to his satisfaction. Yet throughout I had been deeply conscious of the keen and critical scrutiny of my fanciful creations by Leloir, the preeminent authority of seventeenth-century France. So, perhaps, when all was said and done, his absolution was the ultimate balm to my soul, assuring me that I had not been guilty of architectural solecisms.

Plusieurs artistes décorateurs ont à la fois la commande du même décor. Laurence Irving, le petit-fils du grand tragedien anglais en créa de fort important. . . . Ainsi se dressa le château de Saint-Germain-en-Laye, non celui qui abrite le musée des antiquités, mais celui construit par Henri IV et dont il ne reste qu'un pavillon devenu restaurant. Irving dut créer un château de toutes pièces, ce dont d'ailleurs, il s'acquitta merveilleusement. On eût été à Paris, on eût, sans doute, trouve à la Bibliothèque les plans et l'elevation désirés, mais les demander les est fait parvenir, comme on dit ainsi que la moutarde après le dîner. Après tout une inexatitude plus ou de moins . . . il faut être philosophe. (*Six mois à Hollywood,* Maurice Leloir.)[1]

This fascinating book, now, I fear, a collector's piece, profusely illustrated by the author, is an invaluable record of motion-picture making in America at that time. Every detail of studio life is precisely described and depicted by one not blind to its follies and incongruities. Nor did Max spend all his days in dalliance. He contributed a study of the then-current techniques of silent and talking film production that must have been welcomed by contemporary French film directors.

The film was to open with the king's progress through the town of St. Germain-en-Laye in his carriage with a mounted escort of musketeers who later have a rendezvous with D'Artagnan at an auberge in the foreground of the scene. I thought that this procession would be more symbolic of regality if it was seen to be descending from the palace looming above it. So at the foot of a narrow street winding downhill I designed a *place* enclosed by a gothic church, timber-framed houses, and shops, such as can be seen in ancient towns in Normandy today, and in the centre of it a fountain to make the "nub" of the composition. After one or two attempts, I produced the effect he needed to make his initial impact on his audiences. Robert whisked it away and set his modelmakers to work on it while I grappled with the interior and courtyards of the palace. When Douglas saw the models he was disenchanted. And so was I. I did not know that, up to that time, sets in Hollywood were built on flat ground. Consequently, the royal descent to the marketplace that I had aimed to suggest was vitiated by the scene being built on one plane. Amid the general consternation, I asked Robert if I could try my hand at a model. He readily agreed and provided the necessary craftsmen to help me. I traced the outlines of my drawing on a sheet of glass, set it up on a bench and fixed a viewfinder in the approximate position of the camera. As we built up the model to match the tracing on the glass, it became apparent that the effect called for an artificial hill about twenty feet high. The problem was solved; the model conformed to the drawing. Robert, undismayed, deployed his bulldozers (the first I had seen) and gradually the lower half of the set rose from the landscaped ground. He had explained to me that the whole of my elaborate architectural contrivance, including the distant view of the palace that would not be needed as background to the action of the scene, would be represented by a model hung in front of the camera which, merging imperceptibly into the full-scale construction and lit by the same sun, would completely re-alise the spacious effect of my original drawing.

The set occupied about three acres of the lot. The interior and courtyard of the palace were built in full scale. In the foreground of the interior, to enhance the depth of the scene and to convey Louis XIV's passion for hunting, I had drawn a statue of a stag on an imposing plinth. By this time I knew what Hollywood could provide. Sure enough, while the set was under construction, a voluble and accomplished Spanish sculptor was modeling a noble and larger-than-life-size monarch of the royal forests to be cast in plaster. The large areas of marble I called for were covered with sheets of paper printed like lithographs off a tank of water covered with a film of black, blue, and white oil paint that, when stirred, produced tex-tures indistinguishable from the real thing.

Though this film was to be photographed in black and white, I had made all my drawings in colour. Panchromatic negative stock had just be-come available, adding immeasurably to the tonal quality of motion pic-tures. I reckoned that if my sets were coloured accordingly the camera would give a livelier response to them than to the conventional mono-chrome. The result, I think, justified the negligible extra cost.

Soon Robert and I had developed a procedure ensuring that, scenically, Douglas got what he wanted and that I got what I wanted from the team of craftsmen bringing my design to life. Although Allan Dwan was nom-inally director, his contribution was mainly executive, just as Douglas's pseudonym Elton Thomas was a portmanteau title for himself and all those who had elaborated his original treatment of the two novels. Thus Douglas would describe to me his ideas for a scene and the action se-quence it would contain. When he was satisfied that a drawing illus-trated his intention, he would endorse it and, having done so, expect to see it built exactly as I depicted it. If I had any anxiety on this score, it was relieved by the assurance that my work could not be altered by well-intentioned meddlers who were the bane of Hollywood studios. Robert, once he felt that I had graduated from his course of elementary cinemat-ics, gave me the utmost support and encouragement. With a wry smile, but with a gleam of pride in his eyes, he told me that my first set would cost 80,000 dollars. It was a sobering thought that a few light-hearted strokes of my brush in building up a composition would, if they took Douglas's fancy, prove an expensive indulgence.

Once we were underway, the building of sets went forward day and night. Most evenings I returned after dinner to watch vast structures of wood, chicken wire, and plaster rise into the night sky like huge cages il-lumined from within by arc lights. In the world of reality, the architect had the pleasure and often anxiety of watching the translation of his plans into bricks and mortar over a period of several months; I, in this world of make believe, had the ecstasy of seeing the products of my drawing board grow like mushrooms to full stature as at the touch of a magician's wand in as many days. This was a heady experience, and, if mine was not turned by it, it was because my masters had imbued me with values that prevented me from overestimating the virtue of what I was doing. It was, nevertheless, extremely enjoyable—the daily exercise of drawing and the attainment of its ephemeral purpose. I was not, I hope, tempted into meretricious tricks of technique as an easy means to an end acceptable to my employers, whose standards were not necessarily lower but were different from those my training stood for. My nightly patrols though the streets and corridors of my creation brought me into close contact with all the craftsmen at work upon them. From them I learned the meaning of a classless society distinguished, though wealth was unevenly distributed, by its pride in freedom, absence of social prejudice, loyalty to the job in hand, and by extraordinary kindness and amused tolerance towards strangers like myself judged solely on their merits.

Every day brought a fresh challenge. Though the procedure I have described became a routine, now and again I was faced with startling demands. Before my first sets were completed, Douglas asked me to design the exterior of a convent scheduled to be used several weeks hence. He stipulated a window with iron bars some thirty feet above ground with a tree nearby from which a stout branch must be growing exactly fourteen feet from the window ledge and parallel to it. Such were the statistics of the acrobatic feat vital to the success of D'Artagnan's rescue of Constance Bonacieux imprisoned within. Douglas intended to propel himself with a handspring from the branch to the window where, gaining a footing, he would wrench the bars asunder to reach the heroine in distress. A mock-up of these conditions was arranged in the gymnasium. At first he found that about twelve feet, six inches was the limit of his flight. He was confident, however, that in a few weeks he would by constant practice extend it to his target of fourteen feet. I was to build the set accordingly. It was, in the event, the cause of the only altercation we ever had. I thought it wise to plant a shrubbery below the window as a picturesque insurance against accident—the net, in effect, that the most expert trapezists do not deign to rely upon. When he saw the leafy safeguard I had provided, he took it as my lack of faith in his prowess and instantly ordered its removal. Needless to say, he performed this stunt without mishap. Looking back upon the zest that he communicated in his films to his audiences, I believe it was due to his refusal ever to employ a stand-in or stunt man so that the actuality of his fearless acrobatics projected itself from the screen.

Providentially, before I had come to grips with the problems of film design as opposed to the design of film settings, I found a master who revealed to me the fascinating contribution a graphic artist can make to the

precise preparation and forceful presentation of motion pictures. I was
working on the model of my first set when a visitor filled my room with
his amiable presence. He apologised for not having called on me before,
but he had only just returned from his father's funeral in New York. He
was William Cameron Menzies (to rhyme with lenses), the consultant production designer to United Artists. Bill Menzies had been educated at
Harvard and had studied under the well-known illustrator Howard Pyle
at an art school in New York. He had first earned his living decorating
restaurants and saloons. He had married early and brought his bride to
California to seek their fortune. I remembered that Eddie Knoblock had
spoken of him with affection and admiration. For, with his kindly obses-
sion for helping young artists, he had discerned Bill's latent genius and
had persuaded Douglas to engage him as art director for *The Thief of Bagdad*. The grace and imaginative splendour he gave to that oriental fantasy
brought him instant recognition. Though then and thereafter his modesty
prevented him from recognising his preeminence over all other film designers, none, I think, would dispute it.

We became friends at first sight. Our obligations to Eddie were a bond,
and my handling of watercolours in the English style was a professional
credential that he accepted with generous praise. Far from resenting my
intrusion and presumption, as a novice, in making my debut on so vast a
scale, he welcomed me warmly into the fold and offered to help me in any
way he could.

At the outset he advised me not to pay too much attention to Robert's
dogmatic instructions that might lead me to believe that the camera was
the master and not the servant of the designer. He had perfected a method
of projecting his sketches, for those camera set-ups designed to emphasise
the relation of figures to background and to produce an emotional response in the audience, upon plans and elevations from which sets were
built that preserved their distortion and accents of perspective. Thus the
iris of the camera was forced to transmit the designer's intention to its
negative retina. As I browsed over hundreds of his arresting charcoal
drawings in his room above my own, I realised that his method of script
illustration was the most demanding and exciting contribution a painter
could offer to the confusion of talents that too often robbed filmmaking of
any spontaneity. He had proved to a sceptical industry that, with the intelligent collaboration of writer and illustrator, a film could be conceived
on paper dramatically and visually, thereby not only precisely fulfilling
their intention but effecting economies in time that, in terms of studio
overhead, was money.

Bill was ambitious only for scope to exercise his prolific imagination and
technical expertise—so marvellously incorporated in a man of boundless
energy and with a lively dramatic and comic intuition. This ambition was

easily fulfilled. For, even in that philistine stronghold, producers and directors were vying for his services that would inflate their reputations in the eyes of credulous mandarins and undiscerning filmgoers. He had no intellectual pretensions. In all things his heart governed his head. He alluded to his pictured sequences vividly transposed to film as "gags," though many with their rhythmic and emotional content were passages of pure poetry. I refer only to Melanie's lamp-lit confinement in *Gone With the Wind*.

Bill's working hours were long and erratic, for, like Sherlock Holmes, when challenged by a problem of deduction (the translation of the printed work onto visual continuity) he would wrestle with it until it was solved. Though he was by nature gregarious and companionable, his happiness and contentment were rooted in his home—a wife, like my Rosalind, sympathetic to his unpredictable enthusiasms, a capable housekeeper, two children the same age as our own and an Aberdeen terrier as black as Belah, their *bonne à tout faire*, who embraced them with a devotion as ample as her maternal bosom.

Though he had inherited the Scottish virtues of industry and common sense, he had, alas, no native capacity for dram drinking. A small tot of whisky of doubtful probity, in that era of the synthetic circumvention of prohibition, would exhilarate him into a state of blissful comicality, as endearing as that of a Shakespearian clown, so that unscrupulous friends would exploit this ingratiating weakness for the hell of it. He was too soft-hearted to say no to anything but a shoddy piece of work. On Douglas's advice I had pledged myself to six months of total abstinence, for the risk of being blinded by wood alcohol was very real in a rebellious society that took a childish delight in acquiring bootleg liquor of any kind from any source. So Bill and I were able to enjoy each other's company in sober hilarity.

Once I led him into temptation only, for both our sakes, to guilefully cheat him of the opportunity to savour limitless gin of impeccable distillation. Knowing he had spent the war at sea as an officer in a U.S. Navy collier, I asked him to join me for lunch in the wardroom of H.M.S. *Diomede* of the Royal New Zealand Navy, then on a goodwill visit to San Pedro harbour. We had recently entertained her officers in the studio. Bill drove me in his car along the devious route from Hollywood to the coast. Fearful of the Royal Navy's reputation for lavish hospitality, I realised that if he succumbed to it the chances of our safe return were small. As soon as we were piped aboard, I managed to convey to the captain that my friend was under strict orders from his doctor to limit his intake of alcohol. Discipline prevailed, and the flow of pink gin was discreetly curtailed. Bill needed no artificial exhilaration; he was in his element swapping wartime yarns, including his vivid eyewitness account of the Battle of Glasgow. While in that port, some of his men on shore leave had been attacked by rowdies from the lower depths of the city—the Gorbals. To see that justice was done with reasonable counterviolence, the following night he led ashore a party armed with staffs. A prolonged running battle with mounting casualties on both sides was ended by the intervention of naval and military police. Honour was satisfied, and Bill was gratified to know that the encounter was now a legend in naval circles.

So, when we parted from our hosts, Bill was intoxicated only by his excess of affection for "limeys" in general and naval ones in particular. He was, of course, inclined to believe the best of anyone. In vain I tried to convince him of his worth to the industry in terms of salary; in that earthy cuckoo-land of inflated rewards, his was by no means commensurate with his unique contribution. Such was his easygoing, good nature that even his admirer, Joe Schenck, took advantage of his liberal diffidence.

Meanwhile, old Leloir was having the time of his long life. His production of costumes, state *carrosses* for king and cardinal, properties, and weapons of every conceivable kind was prodigious. Attended by his devoted staff of interpreters and assistants, the old campaigner was in the thick of the action that, under his orders, was going forward apace in wardrobe and workshops. Douglas and the cosmopolitan trio of musketeers, Porthos played by Stanley J. Sandford, a giant and portly American, Athos played by Leon Barry, and Aramis played by a volatile Italian actor, Gino Corrado, were the first to be dressed and armed for their roles. All of them, and the opposing enemies of the king led by the Count de Rochefort, played by a master of elegant villainy, Ullrich Haupt of the Deutches Theater, were working in costume weeks before the shooting began. At daily fencing exercises they practised the cut and thrust mêlées that would be the peaks of the film's action and would call for expert swordsmanship.

Douglas had shaved his head, the better and cooler to assume the greying locks of D'Artagnan for the weeks ahead. With the bandana he wore to conceal his baldness on formal occasions at Pickfair or on rare sorties to the theatre, he would have passed for King of the Gypsies. Leloir's costume designs for the principals were superb in detail panache, most of them being made in the studio under his direction. The hundreds of costumes for scores of male and female courtiers, regiments of soldiers, flocks of nuns, peasants, and shopkeepers were supplied by the Western Costume Company. Leloir's gallic sense of thrift was offended when he discovered that the dresses made for him in the studio, rich in lace and ornament, cost sixty-five dollars, while each of the *costumes ignoble* as he called the products of the costumiers were rented for fifty dollars apiece.

Every day he left his drawing board to give the cast lessons in deportment and the manners of the court. The dapper little man in his white linen suit soon put his school of actors, actresses, and crowds of extras through their paces in bowing, curtseying, the graceful carriage of padded and long-trained dresses, and the handling of accoutrements. The pupils delighted in their martinet and eagerly obeyed his commands and suggestions. If occasionally his advice was ignored or some out-of-period folly insisted upon by the director, when we met at Andalusia at the end of a long day's work, he would shrug his shoulders and, with a sigh, say, "Comme les enfants!" And, come to think of it, that is exactly what we were—a crowd of happy children making and playing with toys of infinite variety, egged on by the most playful child of all, Doug, the boy who never grew up and who leavened the drab lives of millions of filmgoers who identified themselves with this paragon of romantic heroism.

Ten weeks after I had started work on the film, the lot was thronged with hundreds of extras standing by for the shooting of its most spectacular scene—the procession of Louis XIV and Cardinal Richelieu through St. Germain-en-Laye. The set, to which Leloir had affixed the seal of his approval with explanatory shop and inn signs, was now known as Irving Boulevard and I heard, with excusable pride, that news of it had spread as far as San Francisco. The camera, with its array of models hung in front of it for the critical long shot, was set on a rostrum and shielded from the sun by a canvas booth large enough to accommodate its crew, Allan Dwan and his team of assistants ready, like despatch riders, to control the crowds assembled for hit or miss action.

Wearing Douglas's gift of a Japanese, straw, solar topee, which made me feel like Mr. Pooter on seaside holiday, I stood by entranced as the deserted *place* came to long-expected life. Assistant directors gradually marshalled the royal contingent and the mass of jubilant citizens onto their starting lines. Cameramen had tested the contrast of light and shade and found it satisfactory. I think that this was the most exciting moment of my working life. No doubt the theatre can give a designer deeper satisfaction as a participant, feeling audiences respond to the performance of players to whose task of creating illusion he may have made some contribution. But this hour of consummation of such a huge-scale conception, which had been so long in realisation and depended on the coordination of so many human and mechanical factors, was unforgettable. I could see the little white figure of Leloir darting here and there as he prompted byplay of key groups of citizens, overhauled the period harness of the horses, and installed tradesmen in the shops he had furnished with authentic wares and farm produce. At last reports came in that all was ready and poised for the director's stentorian shout of "Action!" The cameras whirred. A signal transmitted by relays of megaphones to the extremities of the scattered assembly set the procession in motion. Down the incline of the narrow street came the *carrosses* of king and cardinal with their escorts of mounted musketeers. From every window spectators waved and shouted loyal greetings. As the cavalcade debouched into the *place*, the leading files of horsemen clove a passage through the cheering mob that parted to give way, swirled around the canopied coaches, and closed behind them so that they looked like cumbersome ships ploughing through a foaming sea. Barely had the rearguard made its exit through the arched opening of a street opposite the church when the director shouted: "Cut!" The cameras ceased their whirring. In momentary silence we looked at each other in hopeful astonishment. A cheer went up as the cameraman signaled his satisfaction, and such was the feeling of general participation that the crowd took up the cheers, not for the king but for the triumphant success of their multitudinous performance. No Maximilian apparition had shattered our great illusion. The sun in a cloudless sky had passed its meridian. Apollo had served us nobly, illuminating the players, throwing the facade of the church into bold relief, and casting shadows matching to perfection those of my drawing.

The day's work, so long anticipated, so swiftly executed, was done. When we saw the rushes, Douglas declared that the scene had been successful beyond his imagining. The infection of his enthusiasm spread throughout the unit. Surely Dumas was watching us. Like the musketeers, we were all for one; yet the one, I think, knew in his heart that once and for all he was shooting his heroic and optimistic bolt in the face of the world's pessimism.

When it was all over, Douglas, his trainer, Chuck Lewis, an Olympic champion, Earl Brown, and I met, as usual, in the gymnasium to release the tensions of the day's work in a vigorous game of "Doug." Douglas had devised an amalgam of tennis, squash, and badminton that suited his temperament and provided more exercise to the fleeting minute than any game I have known. The court, with its breast-high net, filled the gymnasium. Heavier shuttlecocks and racquets that were a compromise between tennis and badminton rackets speeded up the volleying rallies that, as doubles were the rule, were long sustained. A variation that added pace and drama to the game was that a player, if he could intercept the shuttlecock with his left hand, could smack it up vertically and so into position for a devastating smash. "Doug" called for quick reaction and energy rather than for skill—hence the ability of a novitiate like myself to be accepted as a sparring partner to such aces.

After a steam bath and plunge, I sat with Douglas milling over the successful conclusion of the day's shooting on which so much depended. He had evidently forgiven and forgotten my angry expostulation when, a few days earlier, I found he had authorised some minor alterations to Irving Boulevard without consulting its progenitor. The blood of my forbears was heated by a discourtesy, which, I persuaded myself for the sake of my fellow art directors, called for stern protest. Now I realised with shame that my motives had been mixed. Cables from home told me that our daughter, Pamela, was approaching the crisis of pneumonia—then a hazardous affliction. I could imagine the stress and anxiety that Rosalind was undergoing and that I could not share. Perhaps I had provoked that altercation in the subconscious hope of getting the sack and my passage home. Anyway, I never again had such cause for indignation, righteous or preposterous.

Douglas was in a reflective mood. Sam Goldwyn and Joe Schenck had departed, leaving the air sulphurous with their boasts of financial wizardry in trading human commodities and playing the stock market. He found such talk depressing, indicative of the ruthless exploitation such as he and his fellow film pioneers had not envisaged as the background to their work. Indeed, for all his success, he was often oppressed by the follies of life in general. He broke off our conversation to remind Chuck Lewis that he must give him some more moustache wax to take home.

"There you are," he said with a self-deprecating laugh. "The best known face in the world after Chaplin's, and the matter of greatest moment and one engaging the attention of two grown men is whether or not it will have enough moustache wax!"

I think it was then that I realised he was approaching the end of a road that he had indeed paved with gold, that the grueling task of filmmaking had lost its charm, and that, having a fertile nest egg, he should end his career with the fine flourish our film promised to be. He was, by nature, restless, and year by year he found it harder to exert the self-discipline to submit himself to the grueling traffic of the studio each film demanded. Every morning, as he donned the iron-grey wig and submitted to the makeup man painting the thickening flesh below the chin a deeper yellow to deceive the relentless eye of the camera, his reflection in the mirror tempted him to quit while he was in the prime of life and on the pinnacle of fame.

There were, too, more tangible and sinister omens that should have warned him that the great days of filmmaking he had so exuberantly enhanced were done.

Leloir might well have likened us to infantile ostriches. For there we were, totally committed to a million-dollar silent film production that, had not Douglas willfully ignored the auguries, would never have been made. For scarcely had be begun when the mandarins of Hollywood were stampeded into vying against one another in a cacophony that had no parallel since the curse of Babel. In that New York projection room we had heard the sound of things to come. Apparently, for some time past, the major production companies had been aware that talking pictures were electronically possible. So great, however, was their vested interest in the production and exhibition of silent films that they had undertaken not to make or exhibit sound-films until they could do so to their mutual advantage. One company, Warner Bros., however, on the verge of bankruptcy, rightly or wrongly jumped the gun. Hurriedly confecting a film entertainment with sound synchronised on gramophone records and featuring the comedian Al Jolson, they showed it at their theatre on Hollywood Boulevard. For weeks an unending queue lined up to see and hear *The Jazz Singer*. It was a saccharine affair with nothing to recommend it but its noisy novelty. Nevertheless, the sobbing strains of "Mammy" were the knell of a medium of entertainment that, for the first time in the history of show business, had enabled people of all nations to enjoy the same jokes and emotional thrills which transcended the barriers of language. The empty coffers of Warner Bros. were soon overflowing. Without enthusiasm, the industry they had betrayed faced the daunting prospect of spending millions on the installation of costly equipment in their studios and cinemas. Since the patents, which now included a method of recording sound on the same negative as the pictures, were held by such industrial giants as the General Electric Company, they found themselves at the mercy of an equally rapacious industry. Moreover, this equipment could only be leased on a royalty basis, with the possibility that he who gets a percentage from the piper might eventually call the tune. Gone with the silence were the monopolies they had so long enjoyed.

The American public, with splitting eardrums, forsook their silent idols, many of whom, like Greta Garbo, Vilma Banky, and Emil Jannings were eloquent only in their native tongues. The word, on the other hand, as though there was not enough of it to endure through the working day, proved in itself to be entertaining by night. Later I would hear an audience murmur in ecstasy at the crackle of eggs frying in a pan held, admittedly, by the ravishing and articulate Virginian, Gary Cooper.

At first, we were all too preoccupied to notice the steady infiltration into the studios of young men as strange in appearance and manner to ourselves as the Mongols must have been to the citizens of Greece and Rome. The scouts of an electronic army were solemn and arrogant. Like Jesuits ardent to convert the redskins, they set about the conversion of one of our stages to sound. I noticed trucks discharging daily at its doors loads of electrical gear and great rolls of dun-coloured felt. At last Douglas was compelled to recognise the invasion of his domain by those intent and humourless technicians. When he heard that the stage was wired and blanketed for sound, he took me with him to see what was afoot. That he was dressed and armed as D'Artagnan made our approach more poignant. He paused at the dark entry and said quietly: "Laurence, the romance of picturemaking ends here!"

Our worst fears were confirmed. The studio, where once in its bright and airy space our sets were built and played into the sweet sentimental strains of music with which a little orchestra stirred the emotions of the players, was now dark as Erebus. Draped with brown felt that lined the walls and hung from the ceiling, festooned with wires and the floor littered with serpentine cables and gadgets that looked like infernal machines, it smelt of a tomb and had the stillness of death. Dante might have conceived it as a purgatory for actors, where utterance and gesture were robbed of spontaneity. Demons horned with earphones flitted in the shadows, testing the stubborn resonance of our old playground. And over a pair of intimidated players was the cylindrical image, hung on the end of a long boom, of the god to whom all must bow down and worship—the microphone. Douglas's intuition was not at fault. Filmmaking, as he had known it, would never be the same again. Nor could he evade another crisis that was threatening his peace of mind.

Since Mary had revealed to the reporters of Chicago that she was shorn of her curls, she had pondered deeply on this parting of the ways in her career. Her womanly intuition had told her that sound had come to stay. She had left New York with the talking film rights of a Broadway success, *Coquette*, in her pocket. Quietly and methodically she was preparing herself to be the first silent film star of her calibre to put herself to the test of sound. Her long experience on the stage justified such a risk. Who knows? Perhaps she might win the first award in that class of The Academy of Motion Picture Arts and Sciences.

Paradoxically, while silence still reigned, she and Douglas had been energetic sponsors in the foundation of an association that would put their art on the academic map. Its inauguration coincided with the disruption of the art it was to represent. Bill Menzies and I had together attended the banquet that launched the Academy's crusade to establish absolute standards in a medium that had become vulgar in every sense of the word. It was presided over by Conrad Nagel, whose Nordic good looks and comparative intellectuality had cast him as master of most of Hollywood's ceremonies. The proceedings would have charmed Stephen Leacock. The solemnity of the occasion was marked by a flow of ponderous verbiage and liquor of a doubtful probity with the result that these well-intentioned pomposities reduced Bill and me, too obviously immune to the high-flown exhortations of the mandarins' oratory, to giggles, thus earning the rebukes or our neighbours who thought that the affair was no laughing matter. By the end of the evening the foundations of the Academy were well and truly laid. Handsome endowments were pledged by corporations and individuals. The symbol of excellence to be awarded by the Academy to the industry's artists and craftsmen was displayed like a monstrance to the reverent congregation. It was a statuette in gold plate designed by the executive art director of Metro-Goldwyn-Mayer (Bill and I exchanged incredulous glances) and bore a startling resemblance to Lazarus rising from the grave. It was soon christened Oscar after, I suppose, a lesser one than Wilde, for the form of it would have set him churning in his porphyry tomb.

A few evenings later I found Chaplin in the steam bath and glad of an audience to attend to his diatribe on the destruction of the miming art that he had made his own. He had more reason than any other film actor to resent the intrusion of sound. For he was the first satirist to set the whole world laughing at the visual lampooning of fatuities common to all mankind. His invention and dexterity as a comic genius was the expression of deepseated social convictions that amounted to emotional syndicalism. People of every creed and colour resolved their tensions and prejudices in laughter at his Erasmian clowning in praise of universal folly. In a way he had more to lose than Douglas did, but he had no intention of losing it. He would not join the stampeding sheep. Speechless, he would hold his peace and, as it turned out, his audiences for several years to come. He invited me to continue the conversation over dinner in Los Angeles.

In his car his mood changed. He dwelt bitterly on the falsity and cupidity of women. His wife had recently left him and, with the aid of unscrupulous lawyers native to California, had acquired a sizeable portion of his fortune in alimony. He was finished with women. Henceforward, he would endure his lot, if not in celibacy, with a life unshackled by the galling chains of matrimony. Women, he claimed, were inimical to the life of an artist.

He broke off to tap on the window and told the driver to stop outside an apartment house. He left me with apologies entered the building and in a few minutes returned, ushering a blond and beautiful girl to the car with a courteous gallantry unbecoming to a misogynist. He introduced me to Miss Virginia Cherrill. It soon became clear that her pretty head was not fit for stratagems and spoils or, I imagined, for any deep preoccupation. Like so many other pilgrims she had come from Chicago to Hollywood hoping that her face would prove her fortune. Like so many others she found ruefully that the race was not to the beautiful where the supply of loveliness was greater that the demand. But Chaplin's discerning eye had seen something in her that agents and casting directors had missed. He had already decided to give her a leading part in the film he had just begun to make—*City Lights*. I soon realised that this was not an emotional involvement that might end in tears. He would make of her what Herbert Beerbohm Tree, through great travail, had made of my mother, when he transformed an incorrigibly public-high-school girl into the vulgar and mellifluous Trilby.

Later, when I was dancing with Miss Cherrill I tried to discover if she understood at all what it meant to be chosen as the partner of the greatest player of our time. Clearly she had no conception of her privilege and none of the zeal of an ambitious actress. Perhaps it was her philistine naïveté that recommended her to Chaplin as a malleable pupil. Her performance as the blind flower girl confirmed, in due course, that the fiction of Svengali's creation of the diva Trilby paled beside the reality of Chaplin's sensitive education of this fair maid of Illinois.

Posterity, alas, will have no pictorial evidence of his omnificent genius as a *metteur en scène,* of his mastery of theatrical and cinematic techniques that are the stuff of filmmaking. Only those who watched him at work could grasp the breadth, resource, and limitless tenacity of his creative mind. The characterisations, the gestures, the nuances of expression, the precise and rhythmic cutting of every sequence were the conceptions of his seriocomic inspiration. "The perfect actor," wrote Edward Gordon Craig, "would be he whose brain could conceive and could show us the perfect symbols of all which his nature contains." Such an actor was Charles Chaplin.

With infinite practice and by exemplary rehearsal he conveyed to each of his supporting cast what was required of him or her as a component on which the phrasing of a composed sequence depended. Spontaneous variations and improvisations were tested and developed. The scene coalesced and Charlie, the clown, round whom it all revolved, gave way to Chaplin, the director, who, stepping back while his stand-in expertly mimicked his routine, viewed critically the realisation of his preconception. And, when all was done in the studio, with the hand of a skilled craftsman and with the audience-sense of the old music hall comedian, he cut and recut those rhythmic sequences and so created new cadences whose triumphs would be measured in decibels of the world's laughter.

Like my grandfather, he relied on a number of "table leg" players who frequented his studio like stock company—alive to his purpose and sharing his insistence on perfection. Many of them were on his payroll long after their working life was done. He may have been jealous of the credits to which he was fully entitled, but he was generous in rewards and affection to old professional companions who helped him on his way from the clog-dancing boy of English vaudeville to the best-loved and internationally honoured artist the stage had ever known.

Gradually, Douglas's irrepressible ebullience got the better of him. Possible, after all, romance and the making of talking pictures were not incompatible. Mary's quiet persistence may have shamed him into making a show of defiance. He, too, had won his spurs on Broadway. So our weekends were punctuated with earnest discussions that eventually would destroy their happiness. Their aim was high, and their purpose admirable. Why should they not together make the first film that would give utterance to Shakespeare on the screen? And in colour, too, for full measure? For some time we weighed the pros and cons of *Othello* and *The Taming of the Shrew*. Douglas saw himself as the Moor in the style of his hero, Tomasso Salvini. Desdemona was, perhaps, no teenage tomboy, but why should Mary be typed at the outset of the era of loquacity? Filmgoers had doted on their personal romance. Would they not flock to see them united in holy "bardolatry"? Douglas's readings with overtones of the Italian tragedian were impressive; on the other hand, Petruchio would offer scope for boisterous horseplay. Though I did not notice it at the time, Mary's cautious misgivings were overruled by Douglas's enthusiastic persuasion. She would be the first to endure the cramping restrictions of the soundstage. Let them wait to see how she fared in making *Coquette*. Our debates were serious enough, though, as it turned out, based on totally false premises. Yet, when I promised to help them in this venture, I did not think it likely that I would have to redeem my pledge.

Meanwhile, my immediate task was to devise a "talking" prologue and epilogue to the all too silent *The Iron Mask*, a concession that Douglas was prepared, if not forced, to make for the sake of the exhibitors. I welcomed it as the first chance to put Bill's precepts into practice. He was now working in partnership with the American dramatist Sidney Howard on a film of Bulldog Drummond for Goldwyn's English star, Ronald Colman, who, having made his stage debut in the provocative London production of Brieux's *Damaged Goods* in 1917, was found to have the now priceless gift of tongues. Precision and economy of time were now of greater significance as studio overheads rose exponentially. Bill's method came into its own. Whatever films may have lost on the swings of silence they gained on the roundabouts of a more intelligent appreciation of the art of film design.

I had managed to make one earlier experiment in this direction with surprising results. Our script called for a torture chamber in a dungeon. For this I made a design that was, in effect, a shadowgraph—the play of light on the unornamented surface of a flight of stairs and a wall on which was thrown the monstrous shade of the figures and instruments menacing the victim. Dwan was deeply impressed that such a melodramatic setting could be produced at minimal cost and with little effort on his part. News of it spread through the studio. Goldwyn asked to see the rushes and then let it be known that he would make a bid for my services. Douglas warned me that I would find him an uncongenial employer. I knew what he meant. After we had seen the epic that had to bear the overheads of Max's catastrophic intrusion, I had congratulated Goldwyn on his production and extolled Bill's superb handiwork.

"Ah," he said, curling his lips contemptuously, "I vant you to know that ven the director had finished, it vos a lousy film. Ven he had gone, I tell you, I made all der retakes and dat is vy it is so goot!"

By now my one desire was to finish our film and be home for Christmas. Robert's earlier assurance that if ever I wanted to return to work with him I should be welcome had, though I did not seriously consider doing so, been proof positive that I had lived down my inexperience.

NOTE

1. Several decorative artists were working on the same scheme of decoration. Laurence Irving, the grandson of the great English actor, created one of the most important. He constructed the Chateau of Saint Germain-en-Laye, not the one which houses the museum of antiquity, but the one built by Henry IV, of which there remains only one pavilion which has been turned into a restaurant. Irving had to create a chateau in all its parts, which he achieved quite marvellously. He could have gone to Paris, no doubt, and found all the plans and elevations in the library, but to have built it thus exactly would hardly have filled the purpose. After all, a little latitude here and there . . . one must be philosophical.

FOUR

The guests regularly attendant on Hearst and Miss Marion Davies at San Simeon had done their best to depreciate the social sovereignty of Douglas and Mary by ridiculing them as snobs cultivating only the acquaintance of titled or important people. I have, I hope, disposed of this myth. The fact remained, however, that distinguished visitors to this celluloid principality expected to be entertained by two stars whose notoriously happy marriage was a guarantee of respectability in what they liked to think and, indeed, hoped was a depraved and orgiastic society. A recent scandal had enhanced the disrepute of the film colony. A young actor, "Fatty" Arbuckle, who with Chaplin had been a member of Mack Sennet's troupe of world-famous comedians, had been made the sacrificial scapegoat that propriety demanded. When Douglas, on his European travels had been received by King Alfonso of Spain, the latter's first question had been, "And how is Fatty Arbuckle?" Douglas asked and was granted permission to convey this royal and sympathetic remembrance to a fellow player very much down on his luck.

No doubt San Simeon and not Pickfair might have been the mecca of pilgrims to Hollywood, but, much as they wished it had been otherwise, its master and mistress were not united in even civil wedlock. Though the days were past when the faithful had to turn a blind eye to the concubines of popes, straightlaced visitors from Europe could not condone the irregularities of a newspaper proprietor. So, though often their hospitable duties were boring beyond measure, Douglas and Mary honourably discharged them for the sake of the goodwill that, in the long run, would express itself in terms of receipts at the box office. Two occasions of such official entertaining were comedies in which I played a supporting role.

One day a message was received from Sir Austen Chamberlain, the British Secretary of State for Foreign Affairs, announcing his arrival at San Diego while on a world cruise and asking if he and his wife could stay the night at Pickfair when they visited Hollywood. This was followed by a second and admonitory telegram from Lady Chamberlain; her husband was not in very good health and she would be grateful if the visit could be kept as quiet and informal as possible. I was eager to meet the architect of the Treaty of Locarno, which we had been told three years ago would ensure peace in Europe in my time. It was decided that Chaplin and I should be the only guests for dinner. Douglas, knowing that his friend's anarchic views would not be agreeable to Britain's ultra-Tory politician, insisted that we should avoid political discussion of any kind. Predictably, conversation dragged and likely starters of small talk withered away. Mary did her best to convert her guests to Christian Science, but they were staunch Anglicans and uninterested in science. Chaplin was ostentatiously on his best behaviour and politely said nothing to provoke controversy. The screening of the first four reels of *The Iron Mask* was therefore a welcome diversion. When the lights went up and Douglas had accepted their courteous congratulations, Lady Chamberlain insisted that her husband must retire to bed early and was escorted by Mary to her room. Sir Austen hesitantly allowed her to gain a lead on him, and, when she had gone upstairs, he turned as he mounted the step up to the hall and asked almost pleadingly: "Would you not like to hear the story of Locarno?" Of course we would—as much as he had been burning to tell it over dinner. And so he did, at fascinating length. I remember best his decorous glee as he described how, at a critical juncture in the negotiations, he was determined that the German Foreign Minister, Gustav Stresemann, and the French Minister of Foreign Affairs, Aristide Briand, should dine with him alone and in secret. Having found a secluded lakeside restaurant some distance from the town, he gave the *patronne* to understand that he was arranging an assignation with a lady and that he relied on her discretion. He recalled her chagrin, when, in the event, covers for three were ordered and the guests of this immaculate and monocled English roué turned out to be a pair of bourgeois-looking business men. But the secret was kept, and over that dinner table he had, perhaps, reconciled those traditional enemies and ensured the harmony of the conference table. After he left to join his by-then impatient wife, we sat discussing all we had heard. Chaplin was very subdued. For the first time, he had been led to hope that statesmen could conduct their affairs with a congeniality and humanity not hitherto conspicuous in their protocol-ridden attempts to set the distracted world in order.

Another self-invited guest was the hero of a chapter of Ruritanian accidents worthy of the pens of Boccaccio and P. G. Wodehouse.

Our shooting was drawing to a close when, one afternoon, I was watching with fearful admiration D'Artagnan, in deadly acrobatic combat with the Comte de Rochefort, in his ill-fated attempt to rescue the man in the iron mask. With expert skill, pulling neither cut nor thrust, they fought it out in a sparsely furnished room of a castle, first one and then the other apparently having his enemy at his mercy but failing to give the coup de grace. At last the villain's foil was whipped out of his hand by our hero, who, flinging away his own, hit his adversary over the head with a chair, leaped on him from above and behind, floored him, and trussed his prisoner with a curtain cord—hot and enthralling work while it lasted. Douglas, leaving Ullrich Haupt dazed and exhausted, came over to me only a little out of breath but with enough to tell me sotto voce that he had received a message from King George V's younger son, Prince George, that he was in Santa Barbara and would like Douglas to give a small party for him at Pickfair the following evening. Douglas's first reaction had been to urge the prince not to come. He knew enough of our royal family's strict propriety to reckon that such an excursion might be frowned upon by the lad's parents and that he and Mary would be ill-advised to countenance it. On rapid reflection it seemed, however, ungracious not to entertain the young man who, if he had any spirit, would turn up in Hollywood anyway; and certainly, if he did, he would be more safely bestowed at Pickfair than anywhere else. So he was cordially invited to a reception at the studio the following afternoon and to a dinner-dance in the evening.

What neither of us knew was that the prince was a junior officer in a British battleship lying off Santa Barbara and that his commanding officer had given orders that he was to remain on board. When the prince spoke to Douglas he had, in fact, already left the ship and was absent without leave.

Entertainments at the studio and at Pickfair were hurriedly arranged. I was invited to dinner but asked to be excused on the grounds that it seemed a waste that a chair should be occupied by an English nonentity when it could enthrone a ravishing film star. I would, therefore, be among those joining the party later. That evening I found Chaplin in the steam bath grinning with mephistophelian inscrutability. He had evidently heard the news for he baited me with assertions that man's moral integrity was only skin-deep and that princes of the blood were as frail as the rest of us. I protested rather pompously that noble obligations could not be corrupted by so unscrupulous and subtle a tempter as himself. Two hours later over dinner, we were still at it; when we parted, like de Rochefort, I was disarmed, my battered head rattling with shattered convictions.

The next morning brought ominous signs of what we were in for. Now Sam Goldwyn had brought a French actress, Mlle. X, to Hollywood from the Parisian music hall that was her natural habitat. Talking films would make her a mute liability. Any opportunity to exploit her for publicity purposes would be welcome. She had already cabled to Prince George, reminded him of their earlier acquaintance (real or imagined), and urged him to ring her up. Douglas had no doubt whatever that she had been prompted to do so by the egregious Sam and decided that on no account must she be invited to the party. But it was too late—she already had the invitation and refused to accept its withdrawal or even to answer the telephone. While we were still trying to confound Sam's knavish tricks, three men were shown into Robert's office; one of them was introduced by his American companions as His Royal Highness Prince George of England. The gaff was blown; *incognito finito.*

The studio entertainment was indeed fit for a prince. Douglas, in costume, played a short scene before the cameras in Irving Boulevard, and then showed his guests a few tricks of the trade—such as windows made of sugar through which he could leap unscathed and guns that spun cobwebs out of rubber solutions. Meanwhile, behind St. Germain-en-Laye, a rodeo had been hurriedly organised. When Douglas and the prince were seated with their retinues in the portico of a fourteenth century mansion, the show began. Cowboys galloped into the arena, saluted our guest, and then with much whooping and shouting lassoed and rode bucking mustangs and bull-dogged, wide-horned steers in the confined arena which reminded me of pictures of bullfights in the narrow streets of Spanish towns. At one point a maddened bronco made straight for the prince, floundered in the shallow ditch beneath us, and pawed the air wildly with flailing front legs. Douglas leapt up and pushed the prince unceremoniously out of danger. One cowboy in the mêlée was trying to throw a steer. He succeeded but fell with it; there was an audible crack, and then, having roped the beast, he emerged with a broken arm. The cowboys were enjoying themselves as much as we were, swaggering and clowning, with yells and yippees, like small boys with justifiable pride in a magnificent impromptu performance.

Afterwards, Mary, in her bungalow, sedately served tea to the prince, Douglas, and myself. Her guest looked very young to be, as seemed likely, the centre of a diplomatic and disciplinary storm. The walls were thin, and I could hear the sounds of conflict next door where Robert had Goldwyn's executives on the mat to be rebuked for their presumption. Douglas, very wisely, told the prince of this embarrassing affair. Shyly, he agreed that, by letting Mlle. X's invitation stand, the gossip writers might be cheated of a scoop. We parted, after an exhibition game of "Doug," to change for dinner. I feel impelled to give for the record what was, perhaps, the last roll call of the stars from when Pickfair was briefly a planetarium of silence: John Gilbert and Greta Garbo, Chaplin, Mlle. X, Gloria Swanson, Billie Dove—galactic company for the prince and his American friends. Afterwards, these were joined by Ronald Colman, Ramon Novarro, John Loder, Norma Shearer and her husband Irving Thalberg (the prodigious producer at M-G-M), Mary Astor, Lupe Velez, June Collier, and myself.

It was not over when the auxiliaries arrived. I was glad, therefore, to be able to tell Ramon Novarro how much I had admired his performance as

Rupert of Hentzau in the first filming of *The Prisoner of Zenda* by Rex In-gram; physically it remains unmatched. When Mary and the prince led the cortege from the dining room, she presented each of us in turn to her royal guest, though in her charming confusion she forgot several of our names. We were then entertained by a troupe of Hawaiian dancers and singers and by a lady in chiffon who galumphed her way through a *pas de seul* with a balloon—evidently a stooge, for, as she pirouetted out of sight, Chaplin, also in chiffon and with a balloon, took the stage; his parody (with its prophetic motif) ended as he sank gracefully to the floor, the bal-loon descending slowly until, cupped in his hand, it exploded with a re-port as loud as the laughter that greeted his superbly timed gag. His clowning broke the thin ice of our constraint. A band struck up, and soon we were dancing to it informally in the hall. Mary was my partner for much of the time and memorably so, for until that night Douglas had never, since their marriage, allowed her to dance with anyone but himself. Together we chuckled as we watched Mlle. X vainly bowling her hoop at the prince, secure in the arms of Gloria Swanson and clearly unbeguiled by Goldwyn's beautiful stool pigeon. It was two o'clock in the morning when he took leave of Mary, pleading a cold in the head and need for rest; on his heels Chaplin bade Mary a reluctant farewell, and the party soon broke up. Douglas had pressed me to stay the night. For some time, we sat on the end of Mary's bed mulling over the alarm and excursions of the last twenty-four hours and congratulating ourselves that the affair could not have been handled with greater discretion and that their hospitality had, indeed, been princely.

Over breakfast, Douglas and I were relieved to read in the papers only brief and polite references to the royal visit. We were, therefore, the more dismayed to find, when we reached the studio, that the telephone had been sizzling with urgent demands from the captain of the battleship as to the illustrious deserter's whereabouts. Worse still, Robert summoned us to his office, where the distraught British consul (of all things, the grandson-in-law of old English actor-manager Sir Squire Bancroft) told us that the prince had vanished without a trace. The day passed in frantic and fruit-less enquiries; the tension grew, portending the storm that must break when the gossip writers tasted blood. It broke from an unexpected quarter.

I tried to sublimate my anxieties at the drawing board. In the late after-noon the gatekeeper came to tell me that an English sailor was demand-ing admittance and that, perhaps, I had better cope with him. Peering through the window of a car, I saw the flushed face of a choleric gentle-man in no mood for trivial courtesies. Looking me up and down with wrathful disdain, he snapped: "Who are you?"

I gave him my name, regretting that I had no number or occupation that he would understand. Once again, the benign shade of "the antique" hovered near me in my hour of need. "Irving—Irving!" he repeated in amazement as his anger began to evaporate. "Any relation to Sir Henry Irving?"

"Yes. He was my grandfather."

"Good God, he was *my* godfather!" exclaimed my now deflated interrogator. And to the matter more germane, he was none other than Admiral Coleridge to whose care and discipline our errant prince had been committed. Moreover, he proved to be the nephew of the judge with whom I had shared the lodging in Leeds when I had been marshal to his colleague Sir Alfred Lawrence. Here, indeed, was a stroke of luck. The irascible British sailor was delivered into my hands. By the time I had shown him round the studio and had persuaded him that Douglas was innocent of luring his runaway lieutenant to Hollywood and of the decorous revelries of the previous night, the roaring lion was cooing like a contented dove. We parted when news was brought to me that the prince had been sighted heading for Santa Barbara. Immediately, the wrath to come dashed off in pursuit of his quarry.

I found, inevitably, Chaplin in the steam bath, grinning like the Cheshire cat and emanating "I told you so" from every pore. What he told me, beginning with the continuation of the party at "Fatty" Arbuckle's nightclub in Los Angeles and then at Gloria Swanson's home was, I think, largely fiction. But its implications were alarming enough to make us all thank the discreet and lucky stars who had kept that Ruritanian night's entertainment to themselves.

As it turned out, I alone was to suffer pangs of conscience for my share in the comedy. In the early hours of the following morning, I wrote for Rosalind a graphic account of the affair, including Chaplin's Rabelaisian epilogue in proof of his evaluation of human weakness. I had no envelope in my apartment so I stuffed the sheets of my letter in the lowered hood of my convertible Chevrolet. When I reached the studio they had vanished—gone with the wind! For days, nursing my guilty secret and certain that some passerby would have retrieved my despatch and sold it to the highest bidding newspaper, I anticipated every morning its disclosure under banner headlines. But, perhaps because nobody in their right mind goes for roadside strolls in Hollywood, the incriminating documents were never found. Had they been, I would have been justly suspect of having sold my friends down the river.

One evening, I came out of the steam bath to find a stranger swimming in the cold plunge bath. He responded cheerfully to my greeting, clambered out, and, taking two towels, wrapped one around his midriff and with apparent sleight of hand twirled the other round his head, which, in an instant, was crowned with a turban that would have graced a Caliph. I asked him where he had learned such an amusing trick. "With my camel corps," he replied. Camels? He was evidently English—the very model of an old Etonian cavalry officer—tall, handsome, and in manner modest but imperative. Before I could ask him where exactly he had been serving, Douglas joined us and introduced him to me as the Prince of Apulia. While we relaxed and dressed, he told me without Italianate flamboyance but with affectionate pride of the native regiments he had recruited and trained in Tripoli. At Pickfair we found Mary entertaining his wife. At dinner I sat next to this fairytale princess. She was petite, beautiful, and charming, but a brunette, whereas in the immutable tradition of pantomime their highnesses are blonde. She had, I discovered, been before her marriage Anne of France, the last of the Bourbons. Now, to one who had recently staged the accouchement of Anne of Austria and the birth of the ill-fated twin brother of Louis Quatorze, this royal couple seemed to bridge the gulf between the ages of romance and reason. They had all the attributes for the roles they played to perfection—youth, good looks and humour, presumably wealth, health, and patently happiness in the love they shared for each other.

After dinner we went to the amusement park at Venice, the Coney Island of Los Angeles. There, incognito intacto, we spiralled down towers on our backsides, staggered tipsily across heaving floors, saluted uproariously our reflections in distorting mirrors, and soared into the night on great wheels—all the fun of the fair and, in such fair company, an evening of frivolous magic.

Fifteen years later, this prince, fearless and guileless as I knew him to be, as the Duke of Aosta, at his headquarters in a cavern in the mountains of Abyssinia, heard of the destruction of his army, besieged in Amba Alagi by British forces restoring the Emperor of Ethiopia to his throne. Already stricken with illness, he surrendered and died a prisoner for a cause he cannot have espoused and for a regime he must have despised. Such was the miserable denouement of a fairy story that so recently, to an incorrigible romantic like myself, had seemed assured of a happy ending but, as can happen in the realm of nursery supernature, was utterly confounded by the demon Carrabos.

If not the most eminent, the person of the most authentic distinction to visit Pickfair arrived on a Sunday afternoon, unannounced but nonetheless welcome. Bear Valley Charlie might have given his name to the valley, for, huge with rolling gait and a deceptively gentle disposition, he had the restrained power and formidable presence of a grizzly. I should not have cared to dispute the narrow track of his plain ethical code. Though shy, his poise was assured. He had a deep drawling voice, at times a ruminative growl as when he described with a touch of affectionate pride how, in the heat of a domestic tiff, his wife shot him in the shoulder.

As a cowpuncher, he had worked for Douglas in the early days of western filmmaking on location. He was fifty years old and had just been the champion of a rodeo at Santa Barbara, though his frame was stitched together by wires, broken in pieces from successive falls and gorings. He had come to repay a debt which Douglas had long forgotten. Pulling a chequebook from the backside pocket of his pants, with a pencil grasped in his knotted paw, he wrote one with unhurried concentration, from time to time holding it at arm's length to assess it like an artist appraising a drawing. This completed, he handed the cheque to Douglas in return for half a tumbler of straight rye whiskey, which he downed in a gulp, and then stood in silence relishing its fiery progress through his pickled vitals.

Thus mellowed, he began to sing in a rasping but piano basso profundo—songs of his rough calling, the lullabies crooned by cowboys to calm their cattle in a storm or to give rhythm to endless days in the saddle driving the herds. He sang, not lugubriously, but with a proud melancholy. The words of his songs were often Homeric in their primitive poesy. I was entranced by this survivor, a contemporary of the Vachell brothers, of the days when such as he would ride 300 miles to swap yarns with a friend. Once he apologised for not being in very good voice—he had recently been kicked in the throat by a horse. But he sang with slow deliberation that made his heart and not his vocal chords his instrument—of a prairie Chaliapin in nature and with the peasant's deep and primordial emotion.

Soon afterwards I descended from serene highness into a criminal abyss when Douglas, rather to my prudish surprise, introduced me to an eminent crook from Chicago who was acting as technical adviser to the production of a gangster film. He was a cool customer not without charm and with a quiet humour—a confidence trickster by trade. One of his precepts I have never forgotten. He remarked that members of his calling never tried to victimise professional people like myself; only men of business and simpletons who believed that it was possible to get money for nothing.

From him I learned to distinguish between the coarse shades of the underworld—the killers, the brothel and gaming housekeeper, the bootleggers, the protection racketeers, and the strong-arm bodyguards serving the barons of organised vice. Shortly before he left Chicago he had attended a ball given by Al Capone (Scarface), which had lasted three days and nights. The walls of the ballroom were lined by armed men while the guests disported themselves in the middle. Among them, consuming torrents of liquor, were the mayor of the city, its leading lawyers, and chiefs of police. The bodyguards, as I already knew, were not a vain extravagance. Only a week or so before, Capone's alter ego in Los Angeles, a man by the name of Marco, had been shot to ribbons outside the office of a lawyer with whom Bill Menzies was conferring at the time. They had been interrupted by the appearance of a very personable and smartly dressed young man who, apologising for his intrusion, stated his innocent business briefly and left. A few seconds later they heard the rattle of machine gun fire. The lawyer opened the window, looked down into the street, and invited Bill to see the visitor's mangled remains on the pavement below. "Gee," he said. "I knew he was hot—but not that hot!" His young client had been Marco. The price of his assassination had probably been less than fifty dollars.

Unhappily, I had personal experience of the ruthless cruelty of the racketeers. One of my draughtsmen asked if he could have my advice on a personal matter. He was a clean-cut, collegiate young American such as would smile confidently on a trustworthy world from the cover of the *Saturday Evening Post*. He told me that, when temporarily out of a job, he had got mixed up with a gang smuggling Chinese immigrants into California. At first it had seemed a rather romantic and exciting lark. Then he was promoted to be one of the crew of a large motor launch that met the immigrants on cargo vessels outside the three-mile limit. The superstructure of the launch was a large iron cage. "Why the cage?" I asked. "To put the Chinese in." he explained. If a government cutter came into sight, the cage and its contents were jettisoned to sink without a trace. Aghast, I asked him how he could be party to such murderous business. "Well," he said, wistfully, "I suppose the Chinks preferred taking the risk to living in China."

He had, however, come to his senses and left the gang. He thought he would be safe working in the studio, but the racketeers had caught up with him and were threatening to beat him up or kill him if he did not rejoin them. Reformed witnesses were expendable. What could he do? My suggestion that he should go to the police was, I realised, as good as a death sentence. I could hardly believe, as I gazed helplessly at this pleasant youth, skilled at his job and potentially the embodiment of the American ideal, that his life was blighted when scarce begun and probably already forfeit; later, his friends told me that they had lost all track of him.

At last the day came when our merry ménage in Andalusia was dismantled. Leloir and Barry, their work done, were eager for Paris; only Max left Hollywood with regret, an awakening from a dream of fair women, hot dogs, and Coca-Cola to the stern realities of life with his uncle at home. Together Leloir and I had contrived the obligatory musical prologue and epilogue to what was otherwise a spirited and authentic film; both of us blushed for their sentimental content but were unashamed of their visual effect. For the prologue my dear old colleague had designed a tapestry depicting D'Artagnan and his friends armed cap-à-pie; these woven portraits dissolved into their models who, stepping boldly from their background, marched towards the camera to the heroic accompaniment of a male chorus. For the epilogue the corpse of D'Artagnan is discovered lying where he fell in the assault of a stronghold on some royal battlefield; the shades of his dead friends loom on the horizon and sweeping forward resurrect our hero, and together the four jovial ghosts go rollicking into the sunset and to whatever paradise Dumas had in mind for them—"One for all and all for one!" sang a choir of archangels. Before we parted Leloir and I, largely to amuse Douglas, were filmed as a savant and his pupil visiting Aramis, the soldier-philosopher, in his parlour. Needless to say, Leloir, with his gravitas and natural poise, was to the film manor born while I, fidgeting and sickly smiling, appeared as uncomfortable as I felt. The sequence was very properly swept up with other rejected footage from the cutting room floor.

Everyone in the studio gathered round to bid farewell to Leloir, the gallant and tireless fellow-worker who had won their admiration and affection. When Douglas gave him the outward and visible sign of his inward and inexpressible gratitude, a gold watch beyond the dreams of its ascetic recipient, Leloir could not conceal his emotion. The little English he had, or wished to have, failed him. As I watched him staunching his tears, I remembered that day when the measure of his stoicism and simplicity were brought home to me. One morning I woke rather late and was dressing when Max, ashen and blubbering, urged me to come quickly to his uncle's room. The old man lay fully dressed on his bed, alarmingly pale and unable to move one arm. Rather than wait for me to drive him as usual to the studio (and for this I felt much to blame), he had tried to board a moving bus, been dragged off his feet, and had fallen in the gutter. In between spasms of pain he was as brave and pert as a little French general, making light of his misfortune and deprecating our sympathy. I asked him if he had ever broken a limb before. "Ah no—like travelling— I have left it until late in life."

Douglas arrived with the doctor; together they carried him into the Rolls and off to the hospital. He had dislocated his shoulder and fractured a rib, but, in a few days, with his left arm in a sling, he was back at his drawing board.

Until then I had never been in his bedroom. As I looked around I was struck by its contrast with my own, filled with books, bric-a-brac, and family photographs. His was bare as a monk's cell; the only signs of his occupation were the hairbrushes on the dressing table. When I helped the doctor undress him, his threadbare linen bore witness to the frugal disciplines of a lifetime. He himself had described his departure from Glendale station:

Plusieurs amis m'avaient accompagné à la gare. Parmi eux Laurence Irving. Avec son amusant humour anglais il me dit: "Vous avez fait la conquête de la Californie. Aux conquérants on remet les clefs des villes. Voici la clef de Los Angeles." Et il me donna une enorme clef doré, sur laguelle autour d'une medaille representant la maison de ville de Los Angeles est écrit: Key to California. (*Six mois à Hollywood*, Maurice Leloir.)[1]

As the train rumbled off to end his long exile, I remembered the comparison he had made between the English and the Americans in the eyes of Frenchmen. Like the Americans, the French found the English friendly but always a little distant. Later he summed it all up: "Bref, les Anglais sont et demeureront nos amis; les Américains peuvent en plus être nos copains." ("In short, the English are and will remain our friends; the Americans can into the bargain be our chums.")(*Six mois à Hollywood*, Maurice Leloir) If, during our companionship, I had shed a little of my native reserve and acquired a little of our hosts' uninhibited cordiality, I hoped I had also found favour in the eyes of this immutable Parisian.

At last I was heading homewards on the "Indian Chief." True, as I shaved on the first morning on the Santa Fe trail, my drawing room was at a standstill and steady as a rock, for the carriage had been left overnight on a siding near the Grand Canyon which Douglas had urged me to explore.

The face I saw in the mirror bore little trace of the metamorphosis I had undergone since I left England. It was plumper and less pallid. Nevertheless, I was looking into the eyes of a different person, their focus deepened by experiences that had effected salutary changes in his whole outlook. He now suspected that the paraphernalia of titles and awards he had been brought up to revere as certificates of "success," even for artists, were now faintly ridiculous. He realised, for instance, that the validity of the Royal Academy lay in the excellence of its schools rather than in the contentious election of its associates and academicians. On the other hand, he was confirmed in the belief held by Ernest Jackson and Charles Ricketts, that the quality of any work that an artist could and should undertake was all that mattered, thus making any distinction between fine and applied art meaningless.

Over the months he had attended places of worship of every Christian denomination with the exception of the Tabernacle of Aimee Semple McPherson, whose radio programmes were sufficient entertainment in themselves, and now realised that the janitors with the keys of paradise were numerous, though each wore a different uniform, and that Catholics and Anglicans had no presumptive knowledge of the theological combination that would open the heavenly gates.

Of more immediate purpose, he had come to terms with the horse. All his life he had been an equiphobe; his fear and distrust of the friend of man had been aggravated when, as a child, he had been dragooned into riding lessons in Regents Park. However, while filming on location, he had, to his astonishment, galloped about fearlessly on a mustang, securely cradled in a western saddle and merely standing in its stirrups for bursts of speed. This, too, confirmed his suspicion that the European cult of horsemanship, with its knee gripping and dressage, was a conspiracy hatched to make riding appear as difficult and dangerous as possible in order to limit the field of huntin' which, with shootin' and fishin', he had imagined was the prerequisite of a knightly order. So it was with confidence that he looked forward to spending the day on the back of a mule—that unprivileged beast born on the wrong side of the horse blanket. No wonder I scarcely recognised my own reflection.

The rocky ground and stark fir trees were powdered with snow when our little cavalcade assembled on the brink of the gigantic rift in the surface of the earth that , perhaps, could be discerned by a man on the moon with a telescope. Our sure-footed mules carried us down a yard-wide track hewn out of the face of a precipice, their rumps in space as they shuffled slowly round each hairpin bend. I had no head for heights, but the exhilaration of the nipping air and the abysmal view cast out fear. I was momentarily panic-stricken when a German woman ahead of me screamed "Ach der precipitismus!" or words to that effect, turned in her saddle, and clung to the ears of my mule who, like his colleague underneath her, stood patiently while the leading guide and I strove to calm her, at the same time sternly reminding her that there could be no turning back. Gradually, she recovered her composure and the reins of her mule. By the time we dismounted to eat our lunch in a semitropical oasis halfway down the canyon she was qualified to ride with the Valkyries.

The Colorado River flowing sluggishly through a rocky gorge was something of an anticlimax, for it was turbid and, though far from stripling, no wider than the Thames at Bablock Hythe. It was the atmospheric contrasts of that expedition that I remember with awe—bleak midwinter when we began our descent, a belt of lush green jungle, and a moonscape of sun-baked rock bare of vegetation at the riverside. I had, in a day, ridden the gamut of our earth's climatic and geological extremes.

After all the business of my departure (including a near miss from death in a downtown car crash on my way to settle my account with the United States Treasury) and emotional farewells, I was glad to go into retreat in my steam-heated and far from monkish railway cell. I passed the hours of my solitary confinement reading the local newspapers I bought at every stopping place. These were the kind of journals edited by O. Henry and a generation of brilliant native writers. Each was a vivid sketch of a little town, like Leacock's Mariposa, where most of its citizens lived and died in fulfilment of their modest ambitions. I was touched by their unabashed self-centredness. Politics for them meant no more than the alternating patronage of the Democratic or Republican mugwumps dispensing local appointments to the faithful. They sought no honours or awards other than holding office as Shriners or Knights of Columbus. Their social activities were as lively as those of Mayfair and recorded with the same gravity, though with less restraint, as those on the court page of *The Times*. When I read the lyrical report of the betrothal of Miss Letitia J. Kalumet of Grant Springs in the *Capello Valley Sentinel*, I thought of the portraits of affianced debutantes weekly adorning the front page of *Country Life* and concluded that, though the latter might regard her New Mexican cousin as uncouth, both were of one mind in the simple hope of living happily ever afterwards. No doubt these plain folk of the Midwest were no great shakes on culture, but it was for their entertainment that I had been working for so many months, and on the whole their idea of a good film was much the same as that of most Londoners.

I had no illusions about the American way of life. I had seen the bright and tarnished side of the dollar—the passionate optimism of so many, like Douglas, who believed they were creating a new heaven on earth, being undermined by the hooliganism and corruption of those bent on making a tormenting hell of it. From these wayside newspapers I learned that there was a less seismic social stratum, a stable America immune to the hectoring of Hearst and unintimidated by the sinister operations of gangsters. I was grateful for this glimpse of the confident, sentimental, and romantic small-town dwellers celebrated by Mark Twain and O. Henry before Babbit sowed the seeds of self-doubt on Main Street.

When safely aboard the S.S. *Berengaria* (ex-Leviathan of the Hamburg America Line, the only tangible spoil of war I ever saw), I visited her Turkish bath before dinner. There I found myself shoulder to shoulder, for it was a mini-hamam, with Somerset Maugham and his secretary, Craxton. I had met the master storyteller at the Garrick Club and felt as uncomfortable in his company as he, perhaps, felt in those surroundings. In spite of Charlie Evans's protests to the contrary, he seemed to emanate a chilling arrogance. This may have been the mask of his own unease. Now, cheek by jowl and stewing in our own juices, we generated a lasting antipathy to one another. I was repelled by his mincing cynicism—the quintessence of sophisticated disillusion that had been so markedly absent in my American friends. His expression was that of a collector turning over stones, regarding what he found beneath them with distaste but as grist to the mill in which he ground the frailties of his fellow men and women into appetising fare for his readers. No doubt he found my homecoming euphoria as ridiculous as my unashamed admiration of Americans. I had not the wit to defend my posture with the aphorism that one "cannot gauge the intelligence of an American by talking too him, you must work with him" (as Eric Hoffer wrote in 1950 in *The Passionate Mind*).

What I took for Maugham's diabolism may have been as much an affectation as the cabalistic sign, with its hint of black magic, that was his colophon. This encounter would have meant little to me, and he, certainly, would not have given tuppence for my opinion of him, had it not finally persuaded me that genius can be directed by both beatific and infernal inspiration, that each muse has a duality that contends for the souls of her servants. Meanwhile, journeymen artists like myself, with insufficient talents to excite the possessive attention of any of the nine sisters, could work away happily in a purgatorial playground free to respond, like with laughter, to benign or malign provocation. I could no longer evade this choice. My pilgrim's progress had been beset with admonitory confrontations. Masefield and Maugham were archetypes of magnanimous and mischievous genius. Ricketts had taught me that our skills could be employed honourably and usefully in the service of corporate enterprises. And in George Bell and Douglas Fairbanks I had met two animators with the rare capacity for drawing out of their votaries more than these knew they had it in them to give.

NOTE

1. Several friends had accompanied me to the station. Among them was Laurence Irving. With his amusing English sense of humour he said to me: "You have conquered California. To conquerors we award the keys of the towns. Here are the keys to Los Angeles." And he gave me an enormous gilded key, on which was inscribed, around a medal depicting the town hall of Los Angeles, the words: Key to California.

Laurence Irving portrait, 1928.

Irving with Mary Pickford and Douglas Fairbanks having just landed in New York City in 1927 following their voyage from Europe (press photograph).

Irving family aboard the S.S. *Carinthia* on their way to Hollywood
via New York, 1928.

Douglas Fairbanks on the steps of his Hollywood
beach house with 4-year-old John Irving, 1928.

Design for the exterior of the river castle for *The Iron Mask*
(from the Kevin Brownlow collection).

Design for the interior palace scene for *The Iron Mask*
(from the Kevin Brownlow collection).

Design for the town square set in *The Iron Mask*
(from the Kevin Brownlow collection).

Studio set for the town square scene during filming of *The Iron Mask*, 1929
(from the Kevin Brownlow collection).

Maurice Leloir, costume designer for *The Iron Mask*, standing with the
ladies of the cast for the film (from the Kevin Brownlow collection).

The "famous four" together (from the Kevin Brownlow collection).

Costume design for Douglas Fairbanks as Petruchio in
Shakespeare's *The Taming of the Shrew*.

Studio photograph taken during the concert hall sequence of the film
Moonlight Sonata, 1936, starring pianist Paderewski.

Photo taken during the shooting of *Moonlight Sonata*, 1936, showing the design for the concert hall (from the Kevin Brownlow collection).

Design for the Covent Garden exterior scene, 1937, in Gabriel Pascal production of
George Bernard Shaw's play *Pygmalion*, directed by Anthony Asquith.

Design for the ballroom scene in *Pygmalion*.

On the set of *Gone with the Wind*. William Cameron Menzies, designer of the film, is on the left; before him kneels Laurence Irving, to acknowledge his debt to Bill M. for his instruction on how films should be designed (from the Kevin Brownlow collection).

Laurence Irving, age 74, at the time he was working on his memoirs.
He died in 1988 at the age of 91.

FIVE

When I did the rounds in London, I found I was the object of greater curiosity than I expected. Hollywood was still *terra incognita* to all my friends, except Eddie Knoblock, who regarded it as an inexhaustible source of fantasy and gossip. It did not occur to me to seek employment in our native film industry as a propagator of Bill Menzies's doctrine, for there were no independent film actors or producers to whom I could offer my allegiance and experience. Our studios, such as they were, were in the hands of minor moguls as ruthlessly commercial as their American rivals but lacking their enterprise and technical skills. Before I was transported to Hollywood, I had a glimpse of the ramshackle and cheapjack conduct of our production companies. My sister had played in a film of Charlotte Brontë's *Shirley* with a promising young actor, Clive Brook. Dolly had been her chaperone on location. Both bore witness to the ignorance and ineptitude of the producers, so that I was the more amazed by the amalgam of single-minded purpose, technical discipline, and judicious economy that was the foundation of the Fairbanks, Pickford, and Chaplin enterprises.

Ben Travers should have been the first to hear of my fulfilment of our shared ambitions in moviemaking. He was then firmly established as resident dramatist at the Aldwych Theatre where delighted and loyal patrons had come to regard Travers and Farce as synonymous terms. In a few years he had become the first playwright since Molière to furnish material for a troupe of comedians, each of them so idiosyncratic as to deserve parts tailored to fit them. The cast for *Plunder* was headed by Ralph Lynn and Tom Walls, the former a brilliant exponent of the dexterous comedic style of Charles Mathews père who a century earlier had been the first to base a farcical performance on accurately observed and true presentments of human nature. But now, with *Plunder* evidently in for a long run, Ben was touring Australia as the mascot of the English Test cricket team, a well-earned indulgence of the only enthusiasm we did not share.

So my first visit was to my drawing master at the Royal Academy Schools, Ernest Jackson, who, though shocked by the prodigal expenditure of talent and treasure on an art form, if it could be called such, that depended on mechanical processes, was amused to hear of my architectural spree. He did not betray his pity for my fall from grace; the still unfinished *Piéta* was a gentle reminder of the disparity between fine and applied art. From him I heard disquieting news of Ricketts and Charles Shannon. Some time before I left, they had moved from their studios in Lansdowne Road to Townshend House, a mansion on the corner where Townshend and Prince Albert Roads meet. It was certainly a nobler setting for a make-believe Mæcenas like Ricketts, for whom near-penury was the badge of a self-denial that enabled him to invest his taste, erudition, and slender means on works of art, often to be had for a song. Nonetheless, he appeared, as George Bernard Shaw (G.B.S.) said, to live *en grand seigneur.* Though in its reception rooms the treasures he and Shannon had amassed were displayed to greater advantage, the warmth and intimacy of their old home were never recaptured. Perhaps our days spent with them in the quiet of the keep at Chilham had robbed the Friday evening soirées of their old enchantment. At this time, I learned the dire consequences of their move.

Shortly before I came home, Shannon, while hanging a picture, had fallen on the stairs. For days he had lain unconscious and now was showing only slight signs of recovery. Ricketts, beset by the conflicting opinions of doctors and by male nurses of daunting impersonality, was distraught. At heart, he had known that the outbreak of the war was the knell of a culture on which all his principles as an artist were based. Now, though the hulk of his lifelong companion remained and must be cared for, he had lost his alter ego; the semitone below the keynote in the chord of their harmonious companionship was silenced.

I wrote immediately to Ricketts, unaware that he had begged his closest friends to spare him such condolences. He responded bravely.

My dear Laurence,

It is charming of you to write. I am glad to say that within the last three weeks there has been a real improvement in Shannon's condition but these cases can last a year or 18 months without visible change. I am hard at work on the Gondoliers (of all things in the world) and have found things have turned out better than I anticipated, but my guilty scene-painter has given me the wrong scale measurements for a baroque ceiling I am designing for the palace in the second act and my sketch which measures 4 foot by over two may have to be done over again if am unable to cut it up to make it fit a different shape.

I should love to see you, when next in town do let me know beforehand as Cecil Lewis who at the moment is snoring on my sofa would love to meet you. He is now in talkies and film work; probably going to Germany in a few days and possibly going to America this fall and both of us would like to hear of your American experiences.

Kindest greetings to your wife and your dear Mother.

Ever sincerely yours, C. Ricketts

Cecil Lewis had been the gayest of the dauntless young night-fighter pilots on the airfield adjoining the one I had commanded at Fairlop. When I met him again as a fellow disciple at Lansdowne House, he was his young debonair self, his natural charm and good looks untarnished by the frustrating years he had spent trying to teach the Chinese to fly, the inventors of the kite proving inept at taking flight themselves. He had returned to England to be one of the pioneers of British broadcasting in the crystal and avuncular days of experimentation on Savoy Hill. I soon discovered that he loved and revered Ricketts as a trusted master to whom he could look for guidance in the study of literature and art. The locust war, and the need when peace came to earn a living, had consumed the years when his keen intelligence might have been honed at university. Lewis had a strong mind of his own. He was able, therefore, while assimilating the wisdom of Ricketts's utterances and the tenets of his aestheticism, to reject the archaism that to some extent inhibited his friend's performance as a creative artist. The lively sense of the ridiculous they shared bridged the gap between their generations—their affection for one another being all the deeper for the wit and frivolity of their communication. "He apprenticed me," wrote Lewis, "to this world and inspired in me the desire to emulate . . . suggested themes, subjects, situations; midwived my earliest efforts, advised, criticised; and when the work was presented to the public, and failed miserably, saw always something in it that made me think that I was right and the world wrong, that I had not failed after all." Such graceful and sympathetic patronage is rarely experienced by young English aspirants and suggests Gallic genes in Ricketts's ancestry.

Now Lewis could and did repay the debt he owed his distraught friend. Such brief glimmerings of distraction and relief, which lit the shadowed years that Ricketts had still to endure, were kindled by the compassion and understanding of a comforter wise beyond his years. Ricketts did not live to see the vindication of the confidence he gave to a young writer. Eight years later Lewis, with *Sagittarius Rising,* would anticipate Saint-Exupéry in the first lyrical expression of man's response to adventure in the new element.

When I called at Townshend House I was interrogated closely by both of them. Ricketts smiled and rolled his eyes upward as the naïvetés and banalities of Hollywood were revealed to him. At the same time, I could see that he would have welcomed an invitation to give on his own terms such extravagant rein to his gifts as a *metteur en scène,* and for my part I had no doubt that he would have acquitted himself as bravely as old Leloir. He questioned me animatedly about my septuagenarian colleague whose earlier work he knew and admired. If for a few minutes I helped him to forget his harassments and replace them with visions of a new career in motion pictures I, too, in small measure, did something to redeem my debt to him. His immediate grasp of the principles of film design I had derived from Bill Menzies was expressed that day by his gift to me of a volume containing some of Hokusai's hundred views of Fujiyama. This became my vade mecum. For it was, and remains, an incomparable lesson in the art of focusing attention on the nub of a composition by setting it in a framework of natural, atmospheric, or human features.

Lewis was attentive, for in talking pictures he had seen a new outlet for his talents. He was not, like Ricketts, stirred by the graphic scope they offered. My visit was timely, for he was already cajoling Shaw to let him make a talkie of *How He Lied to Her Husband*. I failed, evidently, to convince him that the filming of a stage production would not attract moviegoers. In the event, his version of this comparatively trivial comedy fell through the cracks. But, unwittingly, he fostered in G.B.S. the illusion that the dramatist was a natural film scriptwriter—of which, nine years later, I and others triumphantly disabused him. Shaw was always amenable to professional logic. When the time came, he cooperated with gusto in making films that would tune the ears of millions to his dialectic.

I never saw Shannon again. He recovered consciousness but not his intellect. He was forever lost to his lifelong friend whom either he did not recognise or regarded with hostility. When I heard this I remembered that, when driving them home one day to Chilham, Shannon, sitting with Rosalind in the back of the car, had confided to her, as if in jest, that once upon a time he had been engaged to be married but that Ricketts had, as it were, been a just but insurmountable impediment. In the twilight of his subconscious existence, he may have been prey to a long-repressed grievance against the dominating personality that had frustrated his youthful emotions.

Thereafter, Ricketts sublimated his grief in work and travel. The commission to stage *The Gondoliers* was a godsend, and his ready acceptance of it overcame any misgivings of my own in accepting an invitation from Mr. Lee Ephraim to design the sets for a musical comedy, *The Five O'Clock Girl*, at the Hippodrome, the headquarters of Moss Empires, a theatrical octopus controlling most of the music halls in Great Britain. Though I had promised myself a year devoted to painting, I could not work out of doors until the spring. So the offer was opportune. How it came about I could only guess. The cast was headed by George Grossmith, who, for years, had been in effect actor-manager of the Gaiety Theatre. In kindly remembrance of his father's affection for my grandfather, he may have talked the Moss emperors into an extravagance that, as far as I knew, he had never indulged in at his own theatre. Though the production called for twelve sets and rapid changes of scene, I remember it only as my introduction to the scene-painting studios of the Harker Brothers.

When my grandfather was serving his apprenticeship as a "walking gentleman" at the Royal Theatre, Edinburgh, he was befriended by a popular character actor, William Harker. Harker had married a sister of John O'Connor, a scenic artist of renown at that time. Their son, Joseph, inherited his uncle's talent. Many years later he became a young assistant to Hawes Craven in the painting rooms of the Lyceum. My grandfather, hearing that he was the son of his old friend, promised to help him in any way he could. When Joseph Harker went into business on his own, he was assured of as much work as he needed for the Lyceum. His studios off the Walworth Road became that last depository of technical skills and devices perfected and handed down by Inigo Jones, de Loutherbourg, Clarkson Stanfield, and Telbin for the creation of enchanting illusions— the trompe l'oeil wrought with distemper paints on acres of canvas to give the stage new dimensions of relief and perspective. Joe Harker had died only recently; his son and partner Phil gave me a warm welcome. He and his brothers Roland and Colin, all masters of their craft, affected a whimsical insouciance towards it. Designers like myself (whom they might justly have regarded as interlopers) were received with grave courtesy and polite consideration that soon gave way to ribald humour and willing cooperation if we proved our worth. But a pompous and miserly manager would be rapidly deflated by Phil's quiet sarcasm, and an incompetent designer might find himself mocked by the exposure of his folly on a huge scale. A morning spent with these brethren was enough to restore one's faith in artistic and political values that were under fire from intellectual and radical snipers. Happily, none of us foresaw that in our time the stage would be stripped of scenery, as we understood it, and that in these studios the great tradition of scene painting would be practised for the last time.

I was unaware that I was accessory to an unhappy schism. Theatrical historians may be at a loss to understand how scenic artists, on whom for centuries the players had relied to dress their stage and to enhance their task of illusion, were displaced by easel picture painters and designers as creators of the mise en scène and relegated to the role of executants. The polemics of Edward Gordon Craig speeded this dichotomy by exciting the imaginations of directors at a time when the art of scene painting was in decline. Playgoers, their wits sharpened by aesthetic adventures in other fields of art, began to weary of conventional scenic realism—a tradition that had flourished as long as masterly men of the theatre built up their stage compositions against realistic settings with selective strokes of the brush of limelight. But vulgar showmen, drenching their stages with the light that the patrons of girl-and-music shows demanded, had forced the scene painters to acquiesce in the tasteless exploitation of their art in order to keep their studios employed. Thus, even the most excellent scenic artists forfeited the respect of the more cultivated directors who were getting a foothold in the London theatre. At home Granville Barker and Basil Dean and abroad Reinhardt and Diaghilev were employing gifted designers to fulfil their purpose with settings shorn of detail and dresses characteristic and decorative, rather than historically correct, which had instant appeal for modern theatregoers. Thus, rather by accident than by intent, I was among the first to make stage design a profession that, with its responsibility to one's fellow artists, was the most delightful and absorbing work that a painter could wish for.

I was watching my scenery take shape in the workshops of the stage-carpenters and receiving colour on the painting frames of the Harkers, when I was faced with a dilemma that called for swift decision. I received a cable from Douglas and Mary asking me to return to Hollywood to design the costumes and sets (in collaboration with Bill Menzies) for their production of the *Taming of the Shrew*. (The film was ultimately shot in black and white.) So, after all, they had settled for comedy rather than tragedy. I wondered whose persuasion had prevailed. Mary was in a strong position; she had, as she had been determined to do, won the Academy Award for her performance in *Coquette*. Speech had proved no obstacle to the Beetle rolling her pile, but Douglas had remained speechless. Their choice was, I felt, a wise one. Only the most priggish lovers of Shakespeare would regard the play as sacrosanct. Douglas would make a zealous and gymnastic "Tamer"; Mary's teenage termagant would graduate as the Shrew. I recalled our Sunday afternoon conferences and my promise, when and if the time came, to join them in their venture. Well, disconcertingly, it had now come. What was I to do?

Apart from my longing to paint again as soon as the curtain had fallen on the first night of *The Five O'Clock Girl*, I had no commitments. The prospect of rejoining my friends and having a hand in a production that, whatever the outcome, would make film history was, indeed, alluring. But another term of exile was not to be thought of. In the few weeks I had been home I came to wonder how my long absence from it had been endurable. Rosalind was recovering from her operation but had been warned not to overstrain her heart; mine certainly would not stand the strain of further separation from her and the children. Yet with Rosalind in her convalescence and Pam at risk through the long winter, I thought of a possible but unlikely solution to this vexed problem. At such times, Dolly, for all her metaphysical abstractions, having so often had to face such professional problems and to make harsh decisions, could be relied upon to consider them in the light of practical and even ruthless commonsense. What, she argued, could be better than for me to return to the work I had so much enjoyed and at the same time to give my family a recuperative and exciting holiday in California. So, hardening my heart, I cabled that I would gladly come but on my own terms, adding an escape clause that transportation must be provided for my whole family there and back again. To my astonishment my conditions were met generously and without demur, and with kindly prophecies of benefits my invalids would gain from a spell of Californian sunshine. I was charged only to bring the prompt book of a recent production of the play in London. Though I laid hands on one I felt, instinctively, that for the health of the film, theatrical presumptions should be ignored.

So Rosalind and I embarked for New York on the S.S. *Carinthia* with our children goggle-eyed and affectionately disciplined by our nanny Eileen Wingrove, the daughter of a bandmaster of the Buffs who, though her life had been spent following his drums, was dazed by the prospect of the glamorous journey before us.

Our reception in Hollywood was memorable. The charm of transcontinental railway travel was its relaxation. So at the end of our first day in Hollywood, having put the children to bed in our hotel bungalow, Rosalind and I were in good shape for the party Tom Geraghty and his family were giving to celebrate our return. It was as well that we were unwearied by travel for, to our astonishment and delight, Chaplin came to greet us—perhaps to Tom's surprise for he was an elusive guest. I had left him with his strong hair sable-silvered in the conception and planning of his new film; now in the execution of it, his curls were raven-black. For a moment Rosalind mistook his gesture for vanity. Her doubt was soon dispelled. Few actors can pass a mirror without an instant's self-regard but Chaplin was one of them.

After supper our talk turned to London and inspired Charlie's recollections of his childhood in Lambeth, a sombre tale enlivened and adorned by cockney cameos in speech and mime. Until the early hours he held us in thrall evoking the curbside characters of the hostile world outside the home, which his staunch mother lovingly and painfully held together for her boys. He gave us, as it were, an unforgettable preview of the first pitiful chapters of a life printed on the sensitised stock of his cinematic memory for selected takes to be published thirty years later.

At the height of the confusion created by the Warner Bros. premature release of talking pictures, Douglas confided to me that he, Mary, and Chaplin had been approached by bankers in New York with a proposition that would relieve them of all financial responsibility for their productions. In return for a phenomenal cash payment, each would undertake to make two pictures a year. The bankers would finance the making of these pictures and would take the profits (or, as was most unlikely, bear the losses) from their exhibition. With the industry in its present state of flux, the proposal seemed attractive. Their future as stars was uncertain in the changing climate of public taste. The deal would ensure their financial security for life and relieve them of administrative anxieties. Later, Douglas told me that Chaplin, whose joint acceptance of the deal was essential, had refused to be party to it. He insisted that the money they received would not be provided by bankers, but by ordinary filmgoing folk to whom they owed the success and independence they were now enjoying. Moreover, he reminded Douglas that none of them could or would make more than one picture a year of the quality their public expected. Douglas had tried to persuade his friend that there were ways of getting round this commitment, but Chaplin was adamant. It was for him a matter of principle, and by sticking to it he prevented the conclusion of the deal. Douglas and Mary were naturally irritated by his intransigence. His rejection of the offer was even more injurious to their prospects than they could have realised at the time. For the bankers were negotiating for three separate pounds of flesh, each of high nutritional value; they would not have condoned the lumping together of two pounds to make a single dish that might prove upsetting to the consumers. Thus, paradoxically, the joint Shakespearian project would have been stillborn.

In the event, Douglas and Mary's collaboration proved their nemesis. Yet the omens were favourable enough. The part of Petruchio should fit Douglas like a skin-tight doublet; Mary had often played the shrew with a heart of gold. They had assembled a strong cast. Shortly before I left Hollywood I had seen at the Biltmore Theatre the American star Kay Johnson, supported by mainly English players in admirable productions of *The Silver Chord* and *The Doctor's Dilemma*. A young actor, Alan Mowbray, was the most convincing Dubedat I have ever seen. Opportunely appearing in Los Angeles at the outbreak of talkies, they found themselves being wooed by rival mandarins lusting for articulate mummers. The combined prestige of Shakespeare, Douglas, and Mary won us the best of them. The choice of Sam Taylor as director seemed ideal for the purpose in hand. As a college graduate he ranked as an intellectual among his largely untutored peers. He had directed the slick and felicitous comedies of Harold Lloyd and Mary's last and most successful silent film, *My Best Girl*. No one was happier than I to hear of his election. He and Bill Menzies and their hospitable wives had made me welcome in their homes as one of their family; however long the hours I should have to spend in the studio, Rosalind and the children would not want for company. Sam's collegiate sense of humour made him an adept and resourceful director of broad comedy; his Catholicism gave him a kind of serene self-assurance that at times took refuge in stubborn logic. He was not the least awed by his assignment, nor was he impressed by the prompt book I delivered to him. He set about scripting the play with imperturbable zeal. Christopher Sly was thrown overboard with the jetsam of any dialogue that held up the action or was reckoned beyond the ken of the "ninepennies"—the groundlings of the movie-houses. Day and night he was attended by two "gag-men"—rude absurdists after the Bard's own heart—with faces like battered bantamweights and an inexhaustible fund of practical comicalities in the Mack Sennett tradition. This should have reassured the salesmen of United Artists dismayed by the task of having to peddle Shakespeare to the exhibitors of the Midwest. I heard one of them beneath my studio window comforting a colleague: "Sure," he explained, "we're making *The Taming of the Shrew*, but we're turning it into a cah-medy!"

Constance Collier, once Herbert Beerbohm Tree's junoesque leading lady and briefly the fiancée of his stepbrother Max, had been enlisted to coach Mary in an already outdated Shakespearian style of elocution. Sam's hostility to the flamboyant and patronising tragedienne was undisguised. He reckoned that she would sap her pupil's confidence and rob her performance of the natural spontaneity that had won the hearts, and now could charm the ears, of her global audience. I was amused to see the full-blown actress, who had shared the honours of His Majesty's Theatre with my mother, enthroned on the set inviting the deference that Sam denied her. As he foresaw, Mary was for a time confused in trying to affect an utterance and deportment in conflict with the stage precepts she had learned from David Belasco. But before it was too late, her common sense prevailed and the brisk clarity of her diction was not muffled by sonorous declarations. Douglas would do no more than superimpose the overtones of his hero Salvini on the lithe ebullience that Robin Hood, Zorro, and D'Artagnan had in common.

Bill and I were soon aware of tensions engendered by the fusion of the Fairbanks and Pickford organisations to handle a production in which stardom was to be shared and expenses equably borne. The rival retinues felt their loyal duty was to guard the interests of their employers. The old, easy relationship between Robert and myself was bedevilled by the need to get their joint approval of my designs in terms of costs. Douglas's signature on a drawing was no longer a laissez-passer.

Bill and I, working together in complete harmony, found it difficult to get decisions on what settings were required and harder still to produce designs that would satisfy three minds without a single purpose. This did not worry me unduly for I was absorbed in the problems of colour photography, delighting contrarily in the values of true blacks and whites it afforded. In my first flush of enthusiasm I made a few blunders. I had based my costume designs on the patterned fabrics of the Italian renaissance. No such materials were, of course, to be had in California. So I set a team of painters to stencilling and painting by hand yards of coarse linen and burlap. The camera mercilessly exposed my subterfuge; richly apparelled players, like brightly plumaged birds, were lost to sight in their technicolour habitat. As it turned out, my insistence on the restrained splendours of the cinquecento was not accepted; an element of chic was preferred that I could not subscribe to. Only a few of my dreams evaded tinsel modifications by a more pliant nonacento designer. I kept (as much as I could) off the studio floor where the morbid atmosphere became increasingly tense with antagonisms. Sam was losing grip and the confidence of Douglas and Mary, whose forbearance with each other's temperamental foibles was being eroded by assiduous Iagos. At times, it seemed as though a mischievous sprite incited Douglas to ruin scenes for the hell of it, in mockery of the medium in which he realised Mary had a professional edge on him. He would not bother to learn his words, relying on huge placards to prompt him from off stage. Happily, I was too expensive a luxury, as Robert explained with some embarrassment, to be kept on the salary list when my practical work was done. Grateful to Mary's accountants for this economy, I left before the bitter ending of a collaboration conceived in laughter and concluded in tears reached its climax.

My own most palpable shortcoming was my failure to dissuade Sam from a solecism that ruined his career. He had ambitions as a dramatist. Now and again to cover a gag or to sustain an action sequence he had interpolated a line or two of his own in the vernacular. Shortly before I left, I discovered that the opening credit titles of the films, while fearlessly advertising Shakespeare, added in bold parenthesis: ADDITIONAL DIALOGUE BY SAM TAYLOR.

I was keenly aware that critics and cognoscenti in England were likely to decry this American encroachment on their dramatic preserves. Sam's claim would evoke a howl of derision. I could not bear to see so innocent a lamb contrive his own slaughter. For hours I wrestled with my friend and with his quick-witted gagmen, stressing the enormity of this folly. It was to no avail. His stubborn and reiterated justification was: "Well, I did write the stuff, didn't I?" Slowly my passionate advocacy in his defence was weakened by the awful but undeniable logic of his argument. So he became the nine-day laughing stock of the sophisticated world and suffered a self-inflicted wound that never healed.

Mary and Douglas, being old troupers and long conditioned to showing smiling faces to their public and their friends however grievous their private anxieties and bereavements, did not betray their growing disenchantment with each other, outside the limits of their studio. Sundays at Pickfair and the Beach House were as gay and homely as ever. Douglas, who had taken valuable studio-time off to reveal to the children the make-believe muddle of deserted streets, truncated facades of palaces, eastern bazaars, and western saloons, two-decker trams, and period locomotives

scattered over the lot, would engage John in earnest conversation, so entertained by his English accent that he came to address him as the
Colonel. Mary made much of Rosalind and Pam. None of us would have
believed that their careers, seemingly so full of promise, were virtually at
an end. Robert, who had borne the brunt of factional disputes in the studio, shrewdly appreciated the dangers inherent in their ill-fated partnership, but held his peace. We parted from them little dreaming that our
lasting friendship with them both would have to survive their separation.

During our stay I was again made aware of the sinister shadow on the
stars and stripes. Every morning Bill called at our bungalow to take Pam
with his two little girls to the Beverly Hills High School. There, Pam was
holding her own, though now and again she returned with wounds received and perhaps deserved for mocking the cosmetics her contempo-
raries lavished on their childish faces or for refusing to salute the American flag. One day Bill arrived, grave and preoccupied. I asked him what
was on his mind. "There is a fiend abroad," he answered. Now to me a
fiend was a denizen of a supernatural world and, if abroad, could only be
visionary. But Bill meant what he said as he sternly warned the children
not to step outside the school until he came to fetch them.

On the previous evening one of the children had disappeared without
a trace. Later her distraught parents had received a demand for ransom.
Without informing the police, the father went to the rendezvous with the
sum required. At the appointed hour a car approached. His daughter was
sitting beside the driver. A hand was thrust through the window and
grasped the wad of notes. The door was thrown open. The child fell out
onto the curb. By the time her father realised she was dead, the car had
vanished. Her eyes, which he imagined had reflected his own relief at her
release, were sightless—their lids sewn open.

The parents of Beverly Hills were aghast. The hue and cry, inflamed by
the press, resulted in the arrest of a young man, Hickman. He was of low
mentality and gave a confused account of the planning and execution of
the crime to which he confessed. He was found guilty and executed. The
affair confirmed Bill's disquiet as to the fundamental evils that threatened
the peace and well-being of his country, the grim realities that mocked the
fervent and almost hysterical insistence by patriotic Americans of their
immaculate way of life. Both of us had felt the hot wind of violence on our
cheeks.

A few years later I was in Manchester for the opening of a play, Priestley's *People at Sea*, directed by Auriol Lee. Her friend Ruth Chatterton, a
distinguished American actress in her generation, had joined her for the
occasion. Over supper, after the dress rehearsal, our conversation turned
to crime. Miss Chatterton remarked that she had covered the trial of Hickman for a Los Angeles newspaper. I disclosed my personal interest in the

case. She then told me that she and other journalists had circumstantial evidence, based on the time and place at which certain relevant telegrams were filed, that Hickman was innocent. Further enquiries led her to believe that the murderer was the psychopathic son of a high official in the Californian judiciary. She deduced that the mentally deficient Hickman had been persuaded by the offer of a large sum of money to surrender himself and to plead guilty with the assurance that soon after his conviction he would be released from prison. The wretched dupe was, of course, left to his fate. I did not find her suppositions incredible.

We came home on a northern route—Seattle, Puget Sound, Vancouver, and Quebec. Through the moonlit night we gazed in wonder from the train at the Mackenzie River, a vein of silver splitting the dark chasm beneath us. It was dusk aboard the liner out of Montreal when Rosalind and I passed over the grave of my Uncle Laurence and his wife lying full fathom five off Father Point in the Gulf of St. Lawrence. The air was chill and vaporous enough to make me shudder at the thought of the premature quenching of hopes and happiness as seemingly inviolate as those we, only ten years younger than they had been, now shared.

In due course Douglas and Mary came to London with the first print of *The Taming of the Shrew*. They were staying with their friends Lord and Lady Mountbatten, who invited us to dinner and to a private view of the film. Most of our fellow guests were the current hangers-on of Lord Beaverbrook. My only friend among them was the maverick Freddie Lonsdale. Inevitably, he introduced me to the imp behind the throne of political power as the grandson of Sir Henry Irving. "Are yer an Amurrican?" snapped the peer of our long-suffering realm. After dinner, Lord Louis, with a kindly perception that I was out of my element, led me away to see something he knew would interest me. He took me up in an elevator to the top landing of Brook House, and there he opened a door onto the stern cabin of the captain of a light cruiser. It was a replica perfect in every detail from the cork-encrusted steel deck beams to the portholes through which I viewed the panorama of the Mediterranean fleet at anchor in Malta Harbour. The stars and the lights of the town and of the ships were reflected in the still water. To have conceived and executed such a transformation of an attic room in London was a measure of the professional zeal of a naval officer, regardless of the rank or wealth that enabled him to indulge this dedicatory fancy. Thereafter, I kept a sharp eye on his career. It seemed to me to fulfil the high expectations a glimpse of his nautical aerie had inspired.

Lord Louis and Lady Edwina drove us to the private cinema on Wardour Street, to find that with remarkable discourtesy most of their guests had abandoned them. Beaverbrook, like Chatterton of Drury Lane, had evidently pronounced that Shakespeare spelled ruin at the box office. I was pleasantly surprised by the film's pace and style. It was as lively a rendering of that knock-about farce as I have seen since and still bears favourable comparison with later Shakespeare movies. There was no denying that Douglas's tenor voice, pitched higher by microphones and knob-twiddlers, to some extent emasculated his boisterous buckaroo portrayal of Petruchio—but the day had not come when phonetic specialists could make baritones out of tenors. Mary was certainly the prettiest Kate in Christendom, waspish and wonderfully forward until, when tamed, she recited the duty of women to their lords with a touch of tongue-in-the-cheek Irish blarney. Film fans did not appreciate the comparative restraint of their hero and heroine. Critics, for the most part, let them off lightly to make game of the misguided Sam's pretensions.

At best, the film had been a bold flourish by two independent stars with a missionary faith in motion pictures as a power for good. At worst, it foreshadowed the end of an era in Hollywood when individual players, secure in their well-earned popularity, could make films of their choice with their own money, unbeholden as champions of private enterprise, to the capricious favours of the movie mandarins.

INTERLUDE

John H. B. Irving

The family reestablished itself into the Black Windmill, and it was a welcome return. Laurence took the train up to London—his first destination, the Garrick Club. There were changes. No longer was the staff totally male. Meals were served by waitresses. Some elderly members' cheeks were inflated with indignation. There were other new elements. The big lunch table sported more well-known publishers. Theatre impresarios were to be seen, though they tended to eat face-to-face at side tables totally engaged in professional discussion. Roland Pertwee, who had acted with H. B. Irving, introduced my father to Alec Rea and E. P. Clift. They had been running the Liverpool Repertory Theatre, but had recently taken over the St. Martin's Theatre in London. They were looking for a new resident designer, and my father filled the bill. He was welcomed by the group's scene painter, Alick Johnstone, who became a great friend and associate in many future theatre projects. From him Laurence learned the frustration theatre technicians experienced when dilettantish designers came to them with impressionistic sketches that made no technical sense. Together, Laurence and Alick became a team that other producers were happy to employ. Following a number of productions at the St. Martin's Theatre, Laurence in 1931 was approached by the impresario Julian Wylie. He had asked Eddie Knoblock to adapt for the stage a new and very popular novel by J. B. Priestley, *Good Companions*. The play was a musical story of a travelling company performing all over the country. Richard Addinsell composed the songs. The cast included Frank Pettingell, Clive Morton, Edward Chapman, Edith Sharp, and John Gielgud. There were two acts and sixteen scenes following quickly upon one another. The scenery had to be changed with great speed in order to keep the story on the move. The show opened in Birmingham for a week. The London first night at the St. Martin's was a triumph. To Laurence's delight, Douglas Fairbanks was in town and in the audience. Unhappily, Mary Pickford was no longer with him. He and Laurence had breakfast together at the Dorchester Hotel, but conversation was constrained. *Good Companions* ran for a year. Wylie took it to New York, but without his designer. Laurence considered legal action, but fortunately he was advised that Wylie could afford costly legal bills and the action might last for months.

By the end of 1932, Laurence had designed seven more productions. They included *Punchinello* by John Hastings Turner. This, he felt, was his best set of theatre designs, but, owing to the loss of the lead player, John Barrymore, shortly before the opening, things went wrong. The replacement was a failure, and the critics condemned the production and its run was terminated

In 1933 Laurence designed no London productions. Life was centred on the Black Windmill. He joined the Whitstable branch of Toc H, a Christian fellowship organization with a membership mostly of those who had served in the war. They met regularly in an old sail loft overlooking the harbour. Laurence introduced them to acting with a production of R. C. Sherriff's *Journeys End* in the parish hall. He continued his work with the Canterbury Cathedral Festival and its supporting organisation, The Friends of Canterbury Cathedral. He designed a new open stage in the Chapter House, which helped to solve the problem of no access doors to the former stage. Financing for the new construction was donated by his sister, Elizabeth, now married to Sir Felix Brunner.

Their mother, Dorothea, had left her Whitstable cottage. She had joined a mystical group called the Rosicrucians. They were a form of feminine freemasonry, but her lips were sealed regarding their deeply held beliefs. Eventually she bought a cottage near Reigate for her and her companion, Mrs. Parker Jarvis. Occasionally she would come to stay at the Black Windmill. In 1933 her Reigate doctor diagnosed cancer. He operated on her and advised a dubious electrical device called an "Abrams Box." The family next heard that she was in a nursing home in Broadstairs in East Kent. Laurence visited her, but her end was very near. She died and was buried with her husband in their tomb at Headington cemetery in North London. In her will there was a gesture that proved that, in spite of the spiritual divergence from her son, she knew and appreciated the things that really made him happy. This was the gift of one thousand pounds to be spent on whatever he wished. His thoughts returned to the shipyards of Whitstable. Dr. Harrison Butler, a leading yacht designer, was commissioned to design the *Dorothea*, a 32-foot single-masted cutter of 11 tons. She was built in Perkins Yard in 1934. I can remember seeing three-and-a-half tons of molten lead being poured into her keel mould. Later she slid down the launchway into the North Sea to an audience of family and friends. Her final destination was a mooring in Cornwall, Falmouth's Penryn River. Each summer we rented a nearby house with a small tidal harbour, from which we cruised to local places like the Helford River estuary. Such are my memories of wonderful summer holidays in the years before 1939. Back in London, Laurence designed three more Priestley plays, *Bees on the Boat Deck*, *I've Been Here Before*, and *People at Sea*. The first of these starred Laurence Olivier and Ralph Richardson and sought to address current world problems. The play was set aboard a redundant merchant ship languishing aground in the River Fal due to international economic depression. Another play he designed, which gave him great satisfaction, was *Evensong* by Eddie Knoblock and Beverly Nichols. It was the story of an opera diva losing her voice, but bearing the loss and decline of her fame with tragic dignity. The star was Edith Evans, whose performance was widely praised. In her dressing room after the first night, Laurence arrived to congratulate her. She was talking to a tall man, whom Laurence mistakenly thought was her husband. He turned out to be a rich, benevolent patron of the theatre. Laurence's mistake was greeted by a cackle of derisive laughter from a young, blond man with cold expressionless eyes. His name was Hugh Beaumont. In the following years he became "Binkie Beaumont," the man who after the war virtually controlled the theatre in London along lines my father found basically unacceptable.

During the last years leading up to the war Laurence returned to film design. Earlier there had been a episode that had turned his attention to other matters. A Garrick friend and playwright, Harold Dearden, had been invited to be the guest of Admiral Sir John Kelly aboard his flagship, the battleship H.M.S. *Nelson*, in Scottish waters. Dearden suggested that Sir John would enjoy Laurence's company in the same way. There had been a mutiny among naval crews in ships based at Invergordon in northeast Scotland. Laurence joined the *Nelson* off Edinburgh and the fleet sailed north undertaking battle exercises on the way. His host was most friendly. At Invergordon the mutineers were called together on a football field. The admiral addressed them thus: "I've brought you here to take a look at me. I know I'm no bloody oil painting, but, in the future when you see me, you'll recognize me as John D. Kelly, Commander-in-Chief of the Home Fleet!" The admiral's performance as he faced the mutineers was highly theatrical and was enjoyed immensely by his guest. The mutiny was resolved thanks to his firmness and understanding. There followed an occasion when H.M.S. *Nelson* dropped her anchor in Falmouth Harbour and the yacht *Dorothea* came alongside. My father and mother were piped aboard and received cordially in the admiral's cabin.

Laurence's last theatre designs before the war were for *The Sun Never Sets*. The play was adapted from an Edgar Wallace novel written in 1911 titled *Sanders of the River*. The book was an imperial romance in colonial Africa. Basil Dean was the producer. He needed the size of the Drury Lane Theatre to contain a large white and black cast and enough space for the dramatic action. At a crucial moment the hero managed to escape by an aeroplane, which, with attendant noise and in model form, flew off into a sky tinted with a backcloth sunset.

For the last two years before the war, Laurence returned to filmmaking, this time in his native land, though the hero of the first was Polish and the producer of the second a Hungarian.

SIX

Meanwhile, as luck would have it, I had been able to keep my hand in by working on one or two films with maverick directors who appreciated the method I had learned from Bill Menzies—that is to say, the illustration of scripts by continuity sketches that predetermined camera setups and compositions designed to intensify the dramatic impact of the image on the screen. In part, this eliminated costly improvisation and by forethought increased the daily quota of screen time "in the can," thereby reducing the already punitive overhead costs that made film production such a hazardous investment.

It was a matter of luck, for at that time the British mass production companies were organised on the same lines as those in Hollywood. No actor or group of independent artists had asserted their independence as producers. I had watched with some amusement Alexander Korda promoting himself as a producer-director and as the begetter of the most up-to-date studios in the country, which studios gave the little village of Denham in Buckinghamshire an echo of the fame that the pioneer filmmakers had won for a ramshackle suburb of Los Angeles. Rapidly he established himself as a mogul of the aesthetic and intellectual perception that his competitors lacked. This surprised me, for when I was in Hollywood he and Sam Goldwyn were the source of jokes, many, no doubt, apocryphal, that added to the gaiety of the community. While Sam's malapropisms made the rounds, the tales of Korda were of the humiliations he suffered at the hands of his domineering wife Maria, which were his only claim to fame. He was, however, shrewd enough to gauge exactly the right moment to leave Hollywood (as he had in escaping there from Béla Kun in Budapest and, presumably, Maria for England). He teamed with his brothers Zoltan, a skilful director, and Vincent, an accomplished painter who would, he often assured me, have preferred life in a Parisian garret to the affluence he enjoyed as Alexander's art director. Together the brethren proved that they had a flair for making films, which were a cut above their rivals in quality and financed by insurance companies that were vulnerable to Alexander's charm and fluency in whatever may be the Hungarian equivalent of "blarney." Unhappily, he had contracted in Hollywood the endemic disease of "multitalentitis," that is to say, the almost psychopathic illusion that the more writers and artists you employ on the preparation of a film, the greater its chances of success.

The turning point in Korda's career was the well-deserved acclaim accorded to his *The Private Life of Henry VIII*, an entertaining satire inspired, though this was disputed in subsequent litigation, by a lightweight biography of the monarch by Francis Hackett. It owed its success to Charles Laughton's bravura performance, as masterly personification of bluff, boisterous, and villainous regality. Whatever Korda's shortcomings may have been, and many of his dupes would have cause to remember them, he was astute in discovering hidden talents and generous in his rewarding of them, as he elevated a generation of young players to stardom. The most sensitive and beautiful film he made was *Rembrandt,* not only for Laughton's deeply moving study of incorruptible genius, but for the settings that were Vincent Korda's handiwork.

His most popular and competently handled films were adapted from works by A. E. W. Mason. It is significant that in that period Alfred Mason and George Bernard Shaw were the only British writers insistent that every sequence of movies made of their books or plays was subject to their approval or veto. Working in harmony with the most accomplished scriptwriter of the day, R. C. Sherriff, Mason was inflexible in exercising his prerogative. While watching the rushes of *The Drum*, a tale of the northwest frontier of India, Mason heard one of his characters, while defending the reputation of a wayward *mem-sahib*, declare: "There are a thousand English women in Peshawar!" Mason stopped the film.

"I wrote 'a hundred women,'" he roared like a wounded lion. "There were *not* a thousand English women in the place!" The sequence had to be reshot.

Once, while on holiday, I received a telegram from Vincent asking me to work on a production. As it happened, I knew that my cousin, Ralph Brinton, was engaged as its art director. I replied that I thought he was already well served. This was the first and last professional skirmish I had with Korda.

The production of a film based on Walter Hackett's play *77 Park Lane* (1931), which had run for a year at the St. Martin's Theatre, enabled me to bring the principles of continuity-illustration to bear on a modern theme with overtones of elegant skullduggery such as Bill Menzies had so effectively done on *Bulldog Drummond*. The director was Albert de Courville, the wartime impresario of the Hippodrome revues, from which came the songs and catchphrases that had helped soldiers to endure their adversities on the Western Front. As a newcomer to moviemaking, he welcomed my preparatory contribution and more or less gave me a free hand to design the action sequences.

On two counts, that long forgotten film is, for me, still memorable. The still-camera man was a youth who immediately impressed me with his earnest approach, not only to his own work, but to every aspect of film production. Anyone mistaking his quiet reserve for diffidence would be misled. His remarks were terse and to the point, the expressions of an enquiring mind. He spent much time sitting in my room assimilating the significance of the sheaves of compositions that the film cameras would be forced to digest and regurgitate on the screen. His name was Michael Powell. I was not surprised when, within a decade, he had become the first English film director to create a screen idiom of his own with entertaining films that bore the stamp of his own philosophy, working in harmony with the designers of his choice to plan and execute with precision his forceful intentions. Another keen member of our unit was a young assistant director with a flair for light engineering. Based on my rather vague mechanical recollections of Hollywood technology, he constructed an electrically driven gun, with which spiders' webs could be spun from a rubber solution. If our use of it in cellar scenes was a trifle prodigal, our exuberance was excusable as we had added a new gossamer dimension to British film production.

Later I met a kindred spirit, W. P. Lipscomb, a dramatist and director for whom I worked on several plays and one film. Many films deservedly cast into oblivion may contain curious gems in commonplace settings. This one included a sequence that film and musical historians may, to their delight, discover in some graveyard of forgotten movies.

We were screening the tale of Colonel Blood's theft of the crown jewels from the Tower of London, with Frank Cellier in the title role being put through all the Fairbankian paces I could contrive (*Colonel Blood*, 1933). The script called for a musical evening at the house of Samuel Pepys. For authenticity's sake we enticed the entire Dolmetsch family from their home in Haselmere to play, in both senses, their parts in it. Elegantly dressed in Carolean style by a newcomer, Elizabeth Haffenden (with whom I would work on many productions distinguished by her genius and practical skills as a costume designer), they played away on their viols, lutes, and recorders throughout a day as pleasurable to all of us in the studio as the evening would have been to Mr. Pepys, perfectly portrayed by Edmund Gwenn.

Another sequence provoked the only altercation I had with Lipscomb in the many months we worked together. The founding members of the Royal Society, under the eye of their Royal Patron, were to see the demonstration of what its inventor claimed to be a perpetual motion machine. John Bryan and I, bearing in mind the materials and mechanical limitations of the period, designed a contraption of impressive proportions and ingenious complexity. When Lipscomb saw it on the set, he chastened our pride in it by protesting that it would not work. In vain we set its cumbersome gears in motion. No, he meant that those motions would not be perpetual. Tempers rose, and I hotly defended its capability while he as stoutly affirmed its inefficiency. Suddenly, the ludicrous futility of our wrangle dawned upon us, and on the audience now assembled on the sidelines of a promising row, and our differences were resolved in roars of laughter.

Lipscomb had the ready inventiveness and fluency as a scriptwriter that would have found inexhaustible expression in television comedy and drama. Alas, the times were out of joint for he did not live to see the burgeoning of that insatiable medium.

In the summer of 1936, I undertook the design of a film that, for me, at any rate, was of some consequence for it led to my role in a production that would make film history.

Once again, the intermediary of fate was Eddie Knoblock. He had been asked by Lothar Mendes, an experienced German director, to write a story that would frame the first appearance on the screen of the most famous of all pianists of his time, Ignaz Paderewski. For Mendes to have persuaded Paderewski to such an enterprise was something of a coup. He had retired some years before, had suffered a stroke, and at the time lived in Switzerland attended by his personal staff, which included his secretary, doctor, valet, and chef. The difficulty of finding a romantic theme to the taste of such a man of culture and the cost of transporting his ménage to London would have been prohibitive had the film's backers not been certain that the film would attract a global public.

Eddie confected a bittersweet soufflé from conventional ingredients—boy meets girl at concert given by an old friend of her family, Paderewski. Boy nearly loses girl to seductive rival in an ancestral forest lodge; boy and girl are reconciled by the magic of Paderewski's rendering of Beethoven's *Moonlight Sonata* and live happily ever after. This sounds trite. But it provided a silver spit on which to skewer the most popular pieces in the master's repertoire. The comedy was heightened by his conspiracy with the girl's domineering grandmother to bring her to her senses, the latter to be played by the doyenne of English comediennes, Marie Tempest, who had, if provoked, a Martian eye as threatening and commanding as Paderewski's—the perfect foil to his majestic presence.

The opening sequence was a welcome challenge. It called for an uninterrupted crane shot starting from the upper circles of a large concert hall with the distant pianist on the platform, the nub of the composition, and closing in on him slowly as he played Liszt's *Hungarian Rhapsody No. 2*, until, for the last few bars, his hands were to be held in close-up.

The tale was set in Sweden. This gave me a free hand and a chance to convey the idea of a style to which contemporary continental architecture might lead. With Mendes's enthusiastic approval of the model, the set was completed before Paderewski came to town.

One morning, I was standing at the top of the sloping gangway between the stalls, when I saw a little party of visitors entering my concert hall, as it were, stage right. It was led by Paderewski, instantly recognisable in his black frock coat and wide-brimmed Panama hat. For the first time I regarded my huge construction with misgiving. It was conceivable, I realised, that this old-timer might take an instant aversion to my fanciful experiment and refuse to play in such antipathetic surroundings. By this time he had reached the bottom of the gangway. With a beating heart I descended slowly as he, with dignified deliberation, ascended the gentle ramp. We met in midflight. His leonine head, with its mane of locks that age had transmuted from gold to silver, turned in critical surmise, his hooded old eyes appraising every detail of what I now felt to be an arrogant folly. Then he put out his hands and, taking mine in them, pressed them warmly. "Oh, my very dear fellow," he said, implying a blessing of my creation. Instantly, I was his liegeman. For weeks to come I sat with him whenever I could, prompting him to draw upon his inexhaustible fund of wisdom and experience. He had, of course, often supped with my grandfather and Ellen Terry in the Beefsteak Room of the Lyceum. As a man of destiny he was cast in the same mould as Henry Irving, who, no doubt, recognised in that handsome young man of genius a spirit kindred to his own.

Mendes and I had found a stranger bond in common. During the war he had been an observer in the German Air Force and in July 1916 was operating from the airfield at Ghistelles near Brussels, while I was with my squadron at Furnes. Comparing dates and recollections we decided that he must have been the gunner in the two-seater aircraft that so nearly shot me down into the sea off Ostend. Perversely, this sinister intelligence enhanced our friendship.

Mendes, now that his star was safely bestowed in the Carlton Hotel, was eager to go into production. Had the insurance companies underwriting the risks of our enterprise known that the once stricken old man was playing bridge with his cronies into the early hours, sustained by brandy in a haze of cigar smoke, their premiums would have soared.

At last, the evening came when I and my assistants were surveying the finishing touches of the plasterers and painters to the concert hall. In a dark corner of the studio stood a concert grand piano in a pool of light from a powerful standard lamp. From a distance I happened to see a figure, distinguishable at first only by a white collar and cravat, glide from the shadows silently as a ghost to the piano, settle down on the highbacked chair before it, and lift the lid of the keyboard. Paderewski, now strongly illumined, was about to rehearse in what he believed to be an empty studio. Invisible in the pitch-dark perimeter of the lamplight, we crept forward and perched like birds on the scaffolding supporting the wild tiers of boxes that would be in the foreground of the next morning's opening sequence. We listened spellbound as the phantom figure with restrained attack but perfect emphasis played through the music for his first performance before the cameras. I noticed, then, that his lower jaw hung pendulous, rhythmically clenched, and relaxed, as though willing his fingers to respond to the emotional accents of his interpretation. The music, crystal clear, flowed into the soundproof studio, filling it to the brim. Paderewski, when he came to the end of the rhapsody, laid his hands slowly on his lap and for a moment bowed his head, as one praying, haloed with a nimbus of floodlit curls, then rose, closed the keyboard, and vanished into the shadows whence he came. His privileged audience did not betray their presence.

The next morning we were all set for the long crane shot that called for perfect timing. The hall was packed with elegantly dressed concertgoers. At the piano sat Paderewski's stand-in while lights and cameras were focused on him. The maestro and his retinue arrived in good time. He was conducted to a small but comfortable, furnished mobile dressing room near the set. Almost immediately from within came a muffled roar of rage. A distraught secretary popped out as anxious assistant directors converged upon him. What was amiss? Much indeed. Normally Paderewski wore on the platform a deep soft collar and flowing cravat of white linen. The sensitivity of the camera demanded that these should be dyed yellow. In her zeal the studio wardrobe mistress had not only dyed but starched them so that they looked like the bizarre neckwear of the circus clown. The hubbub subsided. Luckily a dyed but limp substitute was forthcoming.

A few minutes later, I knocked on the door and was gruffly invited within. Paderewski seemed to welcome my company. He was made up and from time to time glanced nervously at his ochred mask reflected in the mirror. We talked of this and that, until, suddenly, he confided to me his fear that his performance amid the professional players would appear patently amateurish. I tried to reassure him by explaining that he had only to relax and be his natural self before the camera, letting his personality, which for years had held his audiences captive, assert itself as effortlessly on the screen. Self-conscious acting and artificial mannerisms, I told him, were revealed in all their nakedness through the penetrating and unselective vision of the lens. The dynamism of his platform presence would stand him in good stead, and he must believe that his performance would be as authentic as that of his fellow players. He brooded on this for a while and then, in a high-pitched voice that betrayed his age, said, "Ah— I see—to be a film ac-tor one must be in-no-cent."

He took my hand. The audience was over. I had not misled him. As it turned out he dominated every scene he played, even upstaging and disarming Marie Tempest.

I returned to the platform to view the auditorium as he would see it for the first time. My eye lit on the rather shabby, old mahogany chair set for him at the piano—one such as might be seen in the corner of a Victorian drawing room that nobody ever sat in. It looked out of key with its modern setting. Its padded seat was rimmed with a rather tatty fringe. Absentmindedly, I tried to move it. It would not budge. It was made of cast iron—the fulcrum from which the virtuoso exerted the incomparable force and authority of his performances.

For the rest of the set, my curiosity had been aroused by eighteenth-century Swedish architecture of an order that was not derived from pseudoclassicism. I vented it on an elegant manor house in which most of the other interior scenes were played. It was a pleasure not to be haunted by the critical shades of Palladio, Wren, and Nash. To offset this, I designed the hall of a children's schoolhouse in contemporary style with large picture windows overlooking rolling, forested hills. The walls and furniture were in white except for murals painted in the manner of Carl Larsen, a Swedish painter I had long admired. My idea was to isolate the black, boudoir grand piano and, as I presumed, the sable-clad pianist who would play it. I was, therefore, disconcerted when the scene was being shot to see Miss Tempest enter on the arm of Paderewski, who was dressed in white from head to foot. I need not have worried. A cloak of invisibility would not have diminished the emanation of his benign impulse as he entertained the children with a performance of his own minuet.

When work in the studios was safely done, we left Paderewski with the technicians to long sessions recording the pieces that would have to be synchronised with the related film sequences.

We needed locations suggesting a Scandinavian landscape—forests of fir trees and rafts of lumber floating on rivers or lakes. I recalled the morning of November 11, 1918, when amidst the woods and lakes on the rocky hills above Cragside I had heard the swelling sound of church bells and sirens at the hour of the armistice. I wrote to Lord Armstrong asking if we might use that part of the estate for filming in consideration for a substantial and no doubt welcome fee. He readily agreed. He and his wife Cowkie had wisely abandoned Norman Shaw's rambling "castello" for a lodge on the other side of the River Coquet tributary that ran through a deep gorge spanned by an iron bridge, an early masterpiece of the Elswick Works. When I went there on reconnaissance, they welcomed me as of old and were eager to entertain a party of film folk. We arrived in force, and the citizens of Rothbury proved as hospitable to the young players and technicians quartered on the town, whose demands for provisions and services brought the community a season of unexpected prosperity.

With the help of the foresters I had found a fir tree towering above its fellows. To mark the shift of scene from town to country I arranged for it to be thrown, as woodcutters say, so that it fell towards the camera and apparently on the heads of the audience. In the event, at the director's command—"action!"—the camera whirred as the foresters did their work with such precision that the topmost branches lay only a yard or two from where I and the crew were standing. An unnatural silence warned me that something was amiss. The blanched cameramen looked at each other in dismay. Someone had forgotten to reload the film spools. Reproaches would be of no avail. Dispirited, I found another tall tree that was as expertly felled to some effect. Only I would know that we had failed to get a shot of impressive grandeur and that a lusty giant had been laid low to no purpose. Artfully arranged, the lumber floating on Lord Armstrong's little artificial lakes appeared to be moored to the banks of some great Swedish river ready to be borne downstream to the sea.

I believe that *Moonlight Sonata* still goes the rounds of cinema and television screens. Only very rarely does an artist see an early work of his without dissatisfaction and a wistful longing to repair its shortcomings. I know that, if I should see again that plunging swoop of the camera through my concert hall over the heads of the audience to the lilt of Liszt's rhapsody, the architectural features distorted and dissolved as they flow by like those of a cavern under the sea, the distant manikin pianist growing to full stature until only his sinewy fingers are seen in close-up stabbing at and caressing the keys and compassing them so swiftly as to defeat the speed of film, I would be content knowing that at least one essay in my working life had been faultlessly realised.

SEVEN

The filming of *Moonlight Sonata*, with all its musical, physical, and temperamental hazards, was finished more or less on schedule and without any major crises, largely owing to the tact and professional ability of our production manager, Sammy Samuels. He had mastered the technicalities of studio management in the early days of ruthlessly commercial moviemaking. As a senior executive with the Gaumont British Company, which in the silent days had employed many foreign film stars, his good-natured consideration of their needs and sensitivities made him a popular go-between, easing the inevitable tensions between the artists and the sequestered front office. His affected and amused scepticism towards artistic pretensions seemed like the attitude of a compassionate warden of a lunatic asylum towards its inmates. In fact, his affections ran deep and his innate sentimentality was easily stirred.

Not long after we had parted, he came to sound out my willingness to be enlisted in an unusual project, having recommended me to its promoter as a competent production designer. In due course, he took me to a West End hotel where, in a bleak sitting room, he introduced me to Gabriel Pascal.

Pascal greeted me without any of the spurious effusion to which film producers, to gain their ends, were prone. His manner was friendly and direct. I was conscious of his deference towards artists of any kind until they proved themselves frauds and earned his contempt. He was short and stockily built and showed no signs of self-indulgence. His swarthy Magyar features were volatile. When he smiled benignly he revealed an unusually wide gap between his front teeth that is said to indicate the Midas touch. When angered, he seemed to be holding a latent Tartar ferocity in check. He had been brought up a Roman Catholic, and, lax though he may have been, his aspirations and contritions were often laid in the lap of the Blessed Virgin Mary. His displeasure was usually expressed by a deprecatory pursing of the lips, lowered eyelids, and a brow furrowed to meet the straight line of his strong black hair. His bearing, with its assumption of obedience to his wishes, was aristocratic. Though he never wholly confided his origins to me, I deduced that he was the natural son of some Hungarian patrician. An early photograph of him as a young actor in the national theatre in Budapest led me to suppose that as a youth he could rely on influential patronage.

The room showed a few signs of his occupation—an edition of the plays of George Bernard Shaw, a litter of papers on the table, and, standing in a corner, a cavalry sabre. Film folk, seasoned to imposters, dismissed this weapon as a property to support his bogus claim to have been a cavalry officer. As will be seen, I was later able to confound their suspicions. At first meeting he seemed to me so patently authentic that I readily understood how he had won the trust of G.B.S. who had a sensitive nose for counterfeit characters or sentiments.

I will not repeat the story of their first meeting, as often embellished by its tellers. The plain fact is that Pascal came more or less penniless to London, called upon G.B.S., and persuaded him that he was the long awaited disciple of the master ordained by fate to bring his plays faithfully and stylishly to the screen. He had few credentials to offer. He had for years earned a precarious livelihood on the fringes of the European film industry. Shaw recognised a fanatic when he saw one. He was shrewd enough to discern the basic humility and genuine reverence of a man, which in others was only skin-deep arrogance and pride, but here was a foreign devotee who had a more profound knowledge and understanding of Shaw's works than most of the dramatist's fellow countrymen.

When Pascal told me that he had acquired the English and American film rights to *Pygmalion* and the old man's blessing on its production by him, I was not much surprised. When he told me that he had engaged Leslie Howard for Higgins, Wendy Hiller for Eliza, Wilfrid Lawson for Doolittle, and Marie Lohr for Higgins *mère*, I was amazed. Such percipience was near miraculous in one whose experience of the English theatre was so limited, though his master had, no doubt, approved and in some cases prompted his choices. Never, before, or since had the play been so perfectly cast for any medium. There was, too, an element of bravado about it, for, with the exception of Leslie Howard, all the players were more or less newcomers to the screen and their names displayed on the canopies of cinemas here and in America would not attract any fans. Herbert Beerbohm Tree's grandson, David, would make his debut in films as Freddie, playing the part with a debonair charm that left filmgoers to make up their own minds, as far as Eliza's heart was concerned, about the deliberately enigmatic denouement Shaw insisted upon.

Pascal told me that the director would be Anthony Asquith—the only one in England, I thought, with the intellectual perception, sense of style, and technical mastery to stand up to Shaw and Pascal on matters of cinematic principle and hold the studio floor with authority. Now Pascal came to the point. Would I care to join this venture? From all he had heard from Samuels and from Bill Lipscomb, who was writing the script, my method was all he needed to fulfil his vows to his master.

Quite rightly, his beaming smile assumed my immediate acceptance of such a flattering proposition. The deal, he concluded, was already done. I said that I could not imagine a more inspiring assignment but that, before I could commit myself, there might, alas, be an insuperable obstacle. His face fell like that of an abashed schoolboy. Raising his eyebrows and with pursed lips, he asked for an explanation.

I told him that, since the death of my grandfather, Shaw had provoked his descendants by reiteration in the press of the ridicule and denigration with which he pursued his adversary beyond the grave. No doubt he sincerely believed that this ignorant actor had been the enemy of literature, in his vanity denying the stage to dramatists with a social conscience and leaving behind him an established theatrical order that perpetuated the dominance of the theatre by actors as obdurate as himself. After the death of my father, I was left alone to take up the cudgels in defence of my grandfather against Shaw. Whenever he trailed his coat in the press, I had counterattacked as best I could. I was sure, therefore, that, if Pascal was the man of spirit I took him to be, he would agree that I could not enter Shaw's service until, once and for all, this troublesome hatchet was buried. Clearly, Samuels thought I was out of my mind; but the Hungarian was bred to respect affairs of honour. He undertook to convey the challenge and abide by the result of the duel.

The challenge was accepted. I was at a disadvantage, for Shaw's choice of weapons was words and the rendezvous was set for his flat in Whitehall Court where, as a preliminary courtesy, I was his guest for lunch. I remember very little of that meal; he did not serve up our bone of contention but chattered away on supratheatrical topics. Unlike Max Beerbohm I found no refuge from his "celebration" in my hostess; I felt she knew the purpose of my visit and regarded it as an impertinence. I think there was a fellow guest, but I was too preoccupied marshalling my strategic and tactical plans of attack to heed him. I remember irreverently calling to mind "If," a cartoon by George Morrow in one of E. V. Lucas's "shilling nonsenses" suggesting that if G.B.S. removed his beard it would reveal a receding chin.

As soon as lunch was over he bustled me into his study. I was encouraged to suspect he was as nervous as myself. Exercising the privilege of the prosecution, I briefly reviewed the contumely that Henry Irving had suffered at his hands since his rejection of *The Man of Destiny*. Was he really the champion of literature debarred from the theatre of Henry Irving's creation, or had pique been the spur to his continuing baiting of a man who had proved impervious to his ridicule? Was his grievance genuine? Had he ever offered my grandfather a play that measured up to the expectations, however unworthy, of Lyceum audiences or would give rein to the attributes of the great actor they came to see? Could he not understand that he and his imagined adversary were both in their own ways intent upon the elevation of the drama, fellow apostles rather than contending champions of opposing causes? Admittedly the farouche critic, immune to reverence for men of distinction, was beyond the actor's comprehension. But now he himself was a man of distinction, who, had he not been an irrepressible Irishman, would bridle at the kind of mockery to which he had subjected the Knight from Nowhere (an accolade bestowed upon my grandfather by Max Beerbohm).

Several years later, G.B.S. wrote to me: "I was never really fair to him. . . ." I may not have argued to much effect. But, perhaps, as we wrestled through that afternoon it occurred to him that he had been less than his magnanimous self. I had not reckoned with his deep respect for professionalism that would incline him to believe in the sincerity of my mission. He knew, of course, that I was prepared to forgo a unique professional opportunity and its financial rewards as an act, however, quixotic, of filial piety. Though he made a show of sticking to his guns, this consideration had begun to wear on him before our long debate had ended. In the course of it neither of us pulled our punches or conceded the validity of the other's argument. It would be idle to assess the outcome of our encounter in terms of victory or defeat, but I left the field with his promise that never again would he disparage Henry Irving in public. I knew I could trust him, for on that day I had seen, behind the mask that the exuberant iconoclast Shaw wore in public, the lineaments of Saint Bernard who would have gone gleefully to the stake rather than deny the moral principles that were the tenets of his dramatic creed. Though, a year later, he must have been provoked beyond bearing by the fulsome celebrations of the centenary of Irving's birth, he held his peace. Ten years later, when I was writing the life of my grandfather and I asked him to help me in making a fair assessment of their mutual antagonism, he fired salvoes of unregenerate letters at me that at least clarified the cause of his chagrin. But the hatchet, now rusty from forty years of conflict, was buried. That same afternoon I told Pascal of the outcome of our duel. He smiled inscrutably and urged me to get to work on *Pygmalion* as soon as possible.

The consortium of talents assembled by Pascal with almost mystical intuition to do honour to Shaw worked in unusual harmony. This was due, in part, to the way he engaged our amused affection. He could be stubborn, wilful, and exasperating, but we realised that self-aggrandisement was not in his nature and that his egocentricity was primarily a symptom of his zeal to inspire the trust of his hero. Though his command of the English language was erratic, he conveyed his criticism and exhortations in original and often bizarre phrases. If we presumed that he was out of his depth in trying to grasp the characteristic nuances of the London scene or the niceties of its social conventions, be they those of the upper or working classes, we could be brought to a stop by the pertinence of his comments. My first set, which filled the largest stage at Pinewood, was a pastiche of Covent Garden centred on the facade of St. Paul's Church. When it was finished, he surveyed it for a moment or two and then declared: "Not enough pigeon cack!" He was absolutely right. A hasty application of additional guano gave the scene an authentic London impasto.

Familiar as he was with the subtleties of Shaw's text, he would defer to Asquith and the sensitive and reflective players of his generation and give them free hand to interpret their lines with a style and perception that outdated the dramatist's ideas on histrionics. In the event, Shaw was as delighted by their performances as he had been infuriated by those of Mrs. Patrick Campbell and Herbert Beerbohm Tree in the first and probably worst production of the play.

The only serious obstacle we had to face was a chronic shortage of money. Gaby had not Korda's gift for beguiling backers. His pride and assumption that it was an enviable duty to contribute handsomely to this Shavian enterprise alienated financiers accustomed to flattering supplications. Although we made the film for what, at the time, was the very modest sum of £75,000, we worked from hand to mouth not knowing where the next redeemer would be found. At a critical juncture, Samuels learned that one of the most powerful and wealthy mandarins of Wardour Street nursed an ambition to make a speech in Shaw's company. This intelligence was conveyed to G.B.S. He was not then as rich as, later, the success of his films made him. He readily agreed to indulge the ambitious orator's fancy if by doing so he could be cajoled into an investment that would see us through. They were invited as guests of honour to a lunch at Pinewood. Shaw rose slowly to his feet, mumbled a few incoherent words, and sat down. In a minute or two he had earned a hundred per cent of the sum that enabled us to finish our work.

It fell to me to resolve the only issue with which G.B.S. at first stubbornly refused to cooperate. At the outset, all of us but he were convinced that, whereas theatregoers were content to hear Higgins describe Eliza's success when her oral education was put to the test at a polite social gathering, film audiences would expect her triumph to be seen as well as heard. Shaw, therefore, was importuned to write a new scene with suspense as to whether she would come through the ordeal of a diplomatic soirée with flying colours. He could see no necessity for this. As a last resort I was asked to make a series of continuity sketches calculated to persuade him that, if for no other reason, such a sequence would be well-timed in the setting of an elegant embassy as a welcome change from Higgins's bachelor quarters and the Doolittles' slum dwelling. Shaw, as I soon discovered, did not underestimate the importance of attractive settings to his plays. He had an eye for explicit drawings. On this occasion mine overcame his reluctance to write the necessary dialogue—the more readily, as it would provide a part for one of his favourite actors, Esmé Percy.

The success of *Pygmalion* was immediate and joyous. For the first time, English-speaking audiences, having been entertained by brilliant and provocative dialogue, left cinemas with something to think about other than self-identification with romantic or heroic routines. Here was a change from the clichés of hack scriptwriters, conventional characters, and well-tailored rhythms of comedy and suspense that film distributors insisted were the indispensable grist to their box offices. Audiences delighted in an abstract sequence that no producer of the movie establishment would have tolerated—a montage of sounds and symbols evoking the progress of Eliza's elocutary transformation set to music by Honneger. This was Pascal's inspiration. That he had put it in the hands of a young cutter (later, styled editor) of genius, David Lean, was a milestone in the rhapsodic progress of this Hungarian who had a higher estimate of our several capacities (and Shaw's potential as a star in his own right) than we ourselves presumed.

Shaw's film future and our own as a production team depended on the successful exploitation of this success. We looked forward to years of rewarding work under Gaby's amiable, if capricious, supervision, translating the best of Shaw's plays to the screen. Very shrewdly, the wise old dramatist kept Gaby on a leash by granting him the film rights of only one play at a time. This precautionary tactic and our relationship with our producer that precluded dissimulation and flattering pretences checked any tendency to *folie de grandeur* that such a meteoric rise to film fame could have engendered in a lesser man. We could, of course, only exercise this restraint by our recognition of his genuine devotion to his master.

But for some of us this bright prospect was overshadowed by the gathering clouds of impending crisis that we could no longer ignore. Only G.B.S. and Gaby, in their egocentric absorption and contempt for European sabre-rattlers, were immune to such misgivings. Lacking their Olympian detachment from the grim realities of German and Italian belligerence, I found myself torn between the hope of a miraculous change of heart in the makers of violence that would leave me in peace to pursue the craft I had begun to master, and the growing conviction that, if the worst came to the worst, we could not evade the challenge without betraying the dead of my generation who had frustrated the first attempted Teutonic subjugation of Europe.

One evening at home our son John, then thirteen years old, was listening on the radio to the ranting of Hitler at some Nazi rally. He switched off the spate of rhetorical menace.

"I suppose," he said, without emotion, "my lot will be for it in a year or two."

For the first time I realised that another generation of children such as our own were already condemned to a catastrophic conflict in defence of ideals that this time were not as simple and generally accepted as before. Dismayed, I wrote a letter the *The Times*, describing the boy's fatalistic reaction and pleading that everyone of goodwill and a sense of responsibility from statesmen to newspaper propagandists should strive to avert the calamity before it was too late. My futile protest, to save John embarrassment, was signed "A Father." At least it moved the editor to create a precedent by publishing a letter from an anonymous correspondent.

EIGHT

If extrasensory perception is indeed a faculty, my tentative signals that *The Doctor's Dilemma* should be our next venture were sympathetically received by Shaw and Pascal. I had last seen it played by an English company on a tour of the United States that ended in Los Angeles. We shanghaied half of it when casting *The Taming of the Shrew*, among them, Edwin Maxwell whose performance as B.B. would have delighted G.B.S., the part having been written for the brilliant and equally roundabout comedian Eric Lewis. I knew that Gaby would have little difficulty in persuading Shaw that, if the play was to be filmed, it was now or never while the ideal Mrs. Dubedat was at hand in an actress whose talents were as ripe as Shaw's monstrous regiment of women.

Greer Garson had served her apprenticeship with the Birmingham Repertory Company and was beginning to win the admiration of London audiences. Like Wendy Hiller, she had been unknown in Wardour Street until a few months before, when she made her debut as a film actress in *Goodbye, Mr. Chips*. Ironically, Gaby, with Svengaliesque intuition, had coached her for her ordeal by camera. She had a touch of the charm and flamboyant grace of Ellen Terry and her bold textural beauty that won the hearts of Edwardian painters seeking at once a model and mistress in the Elizabethan sense. Moreover, an arts degree at London University had given her a flickering aura of intellectuality bright enough to intimidate those dazzled by her charm into paying court to her intelligence. Though Gaby's judgment was never prejudiced by his sentiments, I think that at the time he was infatuated with her.

Also at hand was the perfect Dr. Blenkinsop in Ralph Richardson; and, in Hollywood, C. Aubrey Smith was awaiting the frock coat of Sir Patrick Cullen to fall upon him. There was a fairly wide choice of box-office-worthy Ridgeons. The road to stardom was open to some young actor who could reconcile, as Dubedat, the spirit of a ruthlessly egotistical artist whom G.B.S. had embodied in the amoral flesh of the rascal Edward Aveling he had drawn from life. Aveling had driven Eleanor, the daughter of Karl Marx, to suicide. To prepare myself for this welcome task, I spent a week or two absorbing the atmosphere of the London Hospital, studying its routines and the technical equipment of its department of pathology, in order that the ultramodern hospital I planned as Ridgeon's environment should be authentic in detail.

Shaw had been persuaded to let the film open with a sequence, set in a Normandy fishing village, in which the audience would be made aware of Dubedat's genius as a painter and of his casual infidelities to the wife who tirelessly promoted his advancement. The performance of painters had seldom been presented convincingly on the stage. Though in his play G.B.S. was not specific as to the style and quality of the painter's work, in the film it would be necessary for me, as I had done in the exhibition scene in *The Laughing Woman*, to give visual proof of it. Louis Dubedat would, therefore, be discovered footloose in France where his true genius and fickle emotions would be excited by motifs made familiar to the public by the Impressionists and by the buxom daughter of his hotelier, who would be ravished by the handsome and eccentric English guest.

At this juncture, Gaby asked me to accompany him to Hollywood. There, he would rent a large house where I would continue to work in peace and together we could collaborate with a well-known American scriptwriter, who could be trusted to take his Shavian responsibilities seriously.

Almost overnight Gaby had been transformed marvellously into a producer who was to be reckoned with as a contestant in the international infighting of moviemakers. Success had not turned his head or hardened his heart. It had, however, nourished his illusions that, as a financier, he was the match of his competitors in that unscrupulous trade. At the outset G.B.S. had insisted on the terms he imposed on producers of his plays in the theatre—10 per cent of the gross takings, shrewdly judging that, whereas "profits" could be manipulated, the takings at box offices were open to inspection. No doubt he would have helped Gaby to ensure that he got a fair slice of the profits, but his disciple's subsequent behaviour suggested that his idolatry fell short of his faith in the master as a financier.

Shortly after the release of *Pygmalion* in the United States, Gaby had gone to Hollywood where he confronted the Metro-Goldwyn-Mayer lion in its den. He was received with the deference due to a producer whose first film of any account would gross three million dollars in their own preserve and at least a million in its home market.

He returned like Moses from Sinai with the equivalent of a mandate from Yahweh—a legal agreement signed in the presence of His Omnipotence Louis B. Mayer and his own lawyer guaranteeing American release for *The Doctor's Dilemma*, the loan of such of their stars as he needed, and 25 per cent of the costs of production. In exchange for the European rights, Wardour Street, in the person of Mr. C. M. Woolf, would provide the balance of financial support. The purpose of our journey would be to hold M-G-M to their bargain and claim, as it were, the surrender of Greer Garson for one film, for, since Gaby's earlier visit, the talent scouts of M-G-M in London had the scent of a potential winner based on her performance as Mrs. Chips. Before Gaby could declare himself, she had been offered a long-term contract and had accepted it. Now he saw himself as a knight-errant, setting out to rescue a damsel in danger of artistic starvation in the ogre's castle, and myself as his faithful and resourceful squire.

We were to sail forthwith in the S.S. *Normandie*. Greer Garson would be a fellow passenger. By the end of the voyage she would, no doubt, be persuaded that to become immediately a Shavian star was worthier of her histrionic and intellectual merits than to submit to the tedious grooming and promotion for which M-G-M was notorious.

In the event, I saw myself less as a squire than as a character, later portrayed by Jacques Tati, with deep preoccupations stumbling from one bizarre situation to another and reacting to them like a somnambulist. No sooner had we boarded the *Normandie* than I was accessory in a typical *imbroglio pascalino*.

Gaby, with Napoleonic presumption, believed that, wherever he was, there for the time being, his whims and interests must be served. Having used the luxurious appointments of the ship as bait to lure me from England, he invited me to join him for a swim before dinner. I arrived fully clad to find the pool empty and Gaby in a multilingual altercation with the attendant who was hosing down the marble floor. He demanded that the pool be filled instantly. The attendant insisted that it had been emptied on the captain's orders. Gaby was indignant. As Magyar and Gallic tempers rose, both became incensed and suddenly grappled with each other. I tried like Romeo to intervene, but ineffectively, for, whenever I closed in to break up the clinch, I was sprayed by the forceful jet from the hose clutched in the attendant's hand playing at random from the reeling and slithering nub of the conflict. Suddenly, reason prevailed. The combatants let go of each other, shook hands with mutual expressions of regret, and ruefully regarded the dripping figure of the mediator. I left them to their reconciliation and a pool of water on the floor of the elevator that bore me to my cabin and a hot bath. Thereafter in the evening, before we dived into the pool, we went to the nearby gymnasium. There Gaby and I fought happily and less uncouthly with épées. He was delighted to find his squire was also a swordsman (years before at an art students' fencing club, I had won a silver-hilted foil) who, barring cavalry sabres, was more or less his match.

Usually we dined with Greer. She and I were a captive but willing audience to the jovial gasconades of our host—for the tales of his adventures, like those of Benvenuto Cellini and as near the truth, never staled.

As we tucked into the delicious provisions of the ship's cuisine, he would rhapsodise on the limitless prospects of all who jumped on the Shavian bandwagon, which with himself at the wheel would bear them rapidly, if recklessly, along the road to fame and fortune. When in martial vein, he would recall the retreat, after the collapse of the Austrian Empire, of his regiment from the Italian front through passes feebly held by the enemy (for whom he had the greatest contempt) and over mountains already in the grip of winter. He was in command of the squadron responsible for the safety of the regimental treasure chest. The only noncommissioned officer he could rely upon was a sergeant who, when drunk, was a brave and biddable trooper but, when sober, hatched mutinous conspiracies to murder his captain and to desert with the gold. On the Brenner Pass he was sufficiently sober to set in motion his plot. Gaby, forewarned, emerged from his bivouac and, naked but for his kepi and sword belt, faced the mutineers and their ringleader and then, like Napoleon at Jaffa on the seventh of his hundred-day spree, ordered them to kill him where he stood in deep snow or, like the good soldiers he knew them to be, let him lead them to their fatherland. Having won their hearts and liberally supplying the sergeant with the spirit of obedience, he led them on to Budapest and in the nick of time became the instrument of Admiral Horthy's suppression of the rebellion of Béla Kun.

For some time past, he had lost faith in the old regime. The moment of truth came to him during the previous winter on the Carpathian front. It was the custom of Austrian cavalry officers to slap the faces of the grooms as they handed over the reins of their chargers. One morning the cold was so bitter that Gaby shrank from this ritual for fear of hurting his hand. The eyes of his orderly filled with tears.

"Are you angry with me, excellency?" he asked, not having received the blow that had come to be accepted as a gesture of approval. Lieutenant Pascal's affections were, on the whole, liberal and compassionate. From that day he found the manners of the military caste odious and degrading.

Sometimes Greer received us in her cabin, where her career and the characteristics of Mrs. Dubedat were vehemently debated. I had the impression that Gaby was deluding himself if he believed he was wooing her to Shaw. She affected an eager, intellectual response to the challenge but was studiously noncommittal when it came to our coming assault on the mandarins to whom she was in fee. These pleasantly intimate sessions reminded me of those that I had shared with Douglas in Mary's cabin in S.S. *Roma* ten years before and at the same time of the totally different relationship to movies of my present companions. Douglas and Mary had been self-assured in their sturdy independence, artistic and financial, from the powerful forces now arraigned against us and on whose patronage the success or failure of our mission depended, because they were autocrats secure in the conduct of their own United Artists organisation. Gaby, though holding aces as Shaw's preferred producer, was in a poker game with merciless players, masters of bluff and intimidation, with an inexhaustible reserve of chips and not above adroit double-dealing. Nevertheless, I shared his conviction that here, at last, was a chance to create an independent production company, free, thanks to Shaw's keen surveillance, from the blighting restraints of vulgar impresarios and with enough dramatic shots in our locker to keep it so for years to come.

Several decks above us in a palatial suite was Mr. Goetz, the M-G-M representative in London. In his baggage were the film cans containing a print of *Goodbye, Mr. Chips*—proof of the charm and talent of the actress he had so astutely captured. He entertained us with the aloof condescension common to his kind. He could afford benevolence, for Gaby could not elope with his prize in mid-Atlantic or be joined to her in holy legal wedlock by the ship's captain. So, for the time being, a mood of wary bonhomie prevailed as the giant's constable and the knight-errant approached their fateful destination.

Nevertheless, though I was being borne westwards amidst the best of everything in engineering, decorative arts, and culinary masterpieces that France had to offer, I could not shake off the deep disquiet of my departure from England. We had sailed off to news that Mussolini had invaded Albania. Daily, the ship's broadsheet reported the growing Nazi menace to Poland and Hitler's hysterical claims to Danzig. Nor was there a hint of any resolute resistance to these dictators. So a fortuitous encounter proved a tonic to my ailing morale—trivial in the scale of democracy's jeopardy, but balm to the egotism of an ostrich artist.

One evening, while promenading the deck before dinner, I heard the sound of a piano being played with unusual brio. I peered through a window into a small music room. At a grand piano sat, as I assumed, a Frenchman, with his back to me absorbed in his brilliant performance. Unnoticed, I crept in and stood leaning against the wall behind him. When the last chords of a piece by Brahms died away and the pianist had sat for a moment or two with head bowed in contemplation, I declared myself, apologised for my intrusion, and thanked him in halting French for the pleasure he had given me. Uncomprehending, in broken English he disclaimed any knowledge of the language. He had been born a Dane and was now a naturalised American. He was not much over thirty, engagingly modest though the authority of his mastery was evident. He was returning to California from a concert tour of Europe. Naturally, our conversation turned to his native movies. He asked me if I had seen a film featuring Paderewski and the wonderful concert hall in which the master had played and had been so much admired by fellow virtuosi. With a beating heart I confessed that I had designed it. He assured me that in the opinion of most musicians the film would prove a historic contribution to the record of pianism. It seemed, at that time, marvellously comforting to know that the portrait of that great old man we had striven corporately to perfect had satisfied those most qualified to appreciate and criticise our intention, and that our struggle to surmount the inherent human and technical problems of its making had succeeded.

We lingered in New York only long enough for Gaby to present his credentials at the court of the east coast moguls of Metro-Goldwyn-Mayer. In Hollywood, I had been taught to regard Mr. Louis B. Mayer, the boss of its studios, as a sovereign in his own right. Now I learned that he was but a satrap to the New York hierarchy and as dispensable as his own employees. Appropriately, Gaby set up his headquarters at the Ambassador Hotel. There, even the omnipotent Nick Schenck, soft-spoken and urbane in contrast to his buccaneering brother Joe, condescended to call upon this rash intruder who, at a stroke, had made the calculated and complex machinery of moviemaking look ridiculous. In his wake came lesser executives in whom his authority was vested. Few of them had heard of Shaw; none had seen or read his plays; now they spoke of him in hushed and reverential terms usually reserved for the illustrious dead. Chief among them was a suave, well-groomed New Yorker who, until recently head of the city's detective bureau, now was responsible for detecting plays and stories with a screen potential. Gaby, with the bravado of a matador, flourished my drawings before his cold and bovine gaze while I, as picador, pricked his hide of self-esteem by compelling his attention to an art director who evidently did not know his place in the ordered scheme of the industry. Gaby certainly bewildered the signatories of the American order; the steady flow of admonitory cables from G.B.S. (though suffering, at the time, from anaemia, his business acumen seemed unimpaired) added to his stature as a negotiator; whether or not our impertinence antagonised them remained to be seen.

Happily, Gaby had as little taste for nightlife as myself. Our days were full, and, usually, we were early abed to recharge the batteries of our bumptiousness for tomorrow's skirmishing. Yet, Sunday, when we ceased our salesmanship, proved to be the most strenuous of all.

In the morning I went to the Episcopal Church of the Heavenly Rest on Park Avenue to attend the dedication of a stained glass window designed by James Hogan, whose son, Edmund, had joined John Bryan as my assistant. There, I was transported instantly to Leacock's Church of St. Asaph's on Plutoria Avenue with its congregation of bondholders from the Mausoleum Club. For such heavenly rest was clearly for the weary well-to-do with ushers in cutaway coats, pew tickets, and every precaution to prevent it from being disturbed by other, ruder ranks of Christian soldiers. This window was a memorial to Herbert Shipman, late bishop of New York and one time chaplain to West Point Military College. This accounted for the service beginning with a procession of cadets in full uniform and wearing shakos, carrying the Stars and Stripes, and singing "Onward Christian Soldiers." The present bishop in his sermon earnestly advocated holy war against fascists and communists but in terms that would inspire his flock to invest in munitions factories rather than physical participation. The window was unveiled, a lovely and magnificent piece of work, its close leading and jewelled intricacies reminding me of Chartres. The cadets sang their college song in close harmony with a rhythmic hint of swing while ushers made a collection of dollar bills. After we had been blessed, thoroughly rested, we drifted out onto Park Avenue to the strains of an organ with stops for harp and bell effects that made the prospect of eternal rest seem almost inviting.

Afterwards, I accompanied Gaby to a tribal enclave for lunch in the home of Mr. Gondor, a great Hungarian patriot, patriarch, and mediator to the Hungarian immigrant population and editor of their vernacular newspaper. Madame Gondor, with the placid temperament and stalwart physique of a farmer's wife, evidently mothered her fellow countrymen seeking refuge in the land of the free from the spreading plague of fascism in Europe. She had cooked to perfection the homely meal and presided over the relays of guests who came, pored out their woes, ate their fill, and departed for others to take their places. After lunch I paired off with a Romanian woman, highly intelligent and with some command of English, who opened my eyes to the insidious activities of Nazi collaborators undermining the few remaining democratic governments in Europe. One young writer, recently escaped from Germany, gave an imitation of Hitler in full spate of malevolent orator—so brilliant that it cast a menacing shadow over the company though they were safely beyond the reach of his persecutions. It was dusk before the Gondors bade the last of their guests Godspeed.

After a bowl of minestrone at a small Italian restaurant, we looked in on New York's latest wonder—Radio City, the megacinema of all time. We took our seats as the lights of the vast auditorium were being dimmed to presage a floor show of heavenly titillation. From behind the curtain eight Virgin Marys emerged held in pink spotlights as, followed by glamour girls dressed as acolytes and holding electric candles, they took up their positions on gangways flanking the stalls. The curtain rose to reveal the steps and altar of a gigantic cathedral made, apparently, of icing sugar. Enter a chorus of candidates for confirmation who, after some evolutions on the altar steps, arranged themselves into the semblance of a huge cross made of lilies. The audience was enraptured. Nor was it disconcerted when, following the exit of the Virgins and their acolytes, the screen was lowered and on it was flashed: WALT DISNEY'S UGLY DUCKLING.

By this time, Gaby and I would not have been shocked if it had read:
MICKEY MOUSE'S LAST SUPPER.

Our damsel, held to her distressful contract, had been spirited away to
Hollywood soon after our arrival in New York and was imprisoned at
M-G-M. Our business done, Gaby took a transcontinental flight in pursuit
of her. I took a heavenly and overdue rest in splendid isolation aboard the
Super-Chief puffing its leisurely way westward along the Santa Fe trail.

NINE

From Glendale station I drove to the address in Bel Air where Gaby had set up his headquarters in a largish, pseudo-Spanish hacienda, as pleasantly bogus in style and construction as the cloistered Garden of Allah where ten years before I had dwelt happily with my French companions. The interior was spacious but gloomy—no fit habitation, I thought, for a temperamental producer alternately subject to Slavonic moods of smouldering rage or resignation to the futility of the human condition. Wandering through it, I found no signs of occupancy until, looking through the open windows of the sitting room onto a sunlit garden and an inviting swimming pool, I saw the waters troubled, and from them arose, like some monstrous otter, the swarthy figure of Gaby, naked. He strode across the lawn to greet me with the beaming smile of a small boy making mischief in a hilarious situation of his own contrivance. With a kind of contemptuous pride in its vulgarity he showed me over his rented domain. It had been the home of the film star Colleen Moore, and, in spite of the cuckoos occupying her nest, we heard the couriers of sightseeing busloads of tourists assuring them that it was still the habitat of her glamorous self.

Finally, he took me to a semidetached wing, bearing the legend Casa Del Amigos, in which I was to be quartered. I could not have been more comfortably bestowed with workroom, bedroom, and bathroom, insulated against the hubbub of grandiloquent prophecy and irascible altercation that were to be the usual *musique concrète* accompanying Gaby's operation rooms. There I could work in peace, emerging only to be an audience for his operatic tantrums or to be urged by his pretty and devoted secretaries to pacify the tumult of his righteous indignation.

I was there to help him prepare the script of *The Doctor's Dilemma*. We agreed upon a daily routine. He had engaged an American screenplaywright of reputation, skilled in his craft with the gravitas of a professor of English literature and without much humour. Presenting him with an edition of Shaw's plays inscribed by their author proved a tactical blunder for it promoted in him a stultifying veneration for the

103

master and an inclination to regard the text of the play we were adapting as a holy writ.

Every morning we set to work at the pool's edge, hammering out sequences with kinetic possibilities. During the afternoon, in the seclusion of Casa Del Amigos, I would illustrate with continuity sketches. Gaby's supervision of our work was fitful. As the spirit moved him, he would take to the water and, as he swam to and fro, would pause alongside us to exhort or correct us, floating on his back and frowning reflectively at his navel.

Over the weeks we produced a workmanlike and lively screenplay; for as the days went by I managed to undermine the specific gravity of my collaborator and to persuade him, like the salesman of *The Taming of the Shrew*, that we were adapting a "cahmedy."

I was slow to realise that Gaby, when withdrawn from us, was nourishing delusions of omnificent and subtle perspicacity, which in the long run would prove fatal to his ambitions. It had occurred to me as strange that Lipscomb, now riding high in Hollywood on the strength of his credit as the screen-playwright of *Pygmalion*, was not our present workmate. I visited him often at his home where his wife was expecting a baby; he appeared to be content under contract to one of the major corporations and not at all eager to reenact the Strum und Drang of reconciling the dramatist and his movie-medium; for Gaby, keenly and often brilliantly intuitive to audience reactions, would use us all ruthlessly as stalking horses to test Shaw's patience with suggestions from which, if they were rejected, he would blandly disassociate himself.

From the outset Gaby, whether or not his heart was engaged, should have realised that his pursuit of Greer Garson was a forlorn hope. The knight-errant and questing beast were ever at odds in him. The giant Metro-Goldwyn-Meyer, hungering after the Jack who had climbed up the beanstalk of *Pygmalion* to eminence as a producer, would use him solely for its own profit. The damsel had become, therefore, a lure that might trap him as a fellow-captive and not as a jewel on loan to adorn the crown of his independence. Moreover she was now chaperoned by her worldly, wise mother, who very sensibly preferred the substantial rewards of a contract in Hollywood to the rhapsodic visions of aesthetic triumphs that depended on the survival of the octogenarian genius of Ayot St. Lawrence.

So while, in daily cables to G.B.S. of inordinate length, Gaby extolled the advantages of American financial backing and the engagement of totally unsuitable American stars, assuring him of the ultimate success of our knight's errantry, answering ones, terse and to the point, warned us that Shaw would not under any conditions commit his plays to the philistines and that Gaby would be left "nakkid" without his patronage if he sold himself in slavery to them.

A subsidiary campaign was being waged to secure the release of *The Doctor's Dilemma* in the United States on terms acceptable to all concerned. Only G.B.S. and those whose timely loans had enabled us to finish *Pygmalion* were making much profit from its success. Gaby had pawned his share of it for cash to see the production through and to pay for such extravagances as our present excursion. In spite of this, he began to see himself, in addition to his other fantastic impersonations, as a wizard of finance. In a week or two he had conducted a single-handed assault on the forces of M-G-M and the United States Treasury—the latter contemplating punitive tariffs to restrict the import of European and particularly British films. Urged by G.B.S. to mind his own business, which was not business, Gaby enlisted the help of an intermediary, allegedly *persona grata* at the White House. This quiet and polite recruit to our cause had recently returned from Germany, where he had been sent by Morgenthau to gauge the substance of the Nazi menace. Presumably, he had assured the Secretary of Finance, as he had convinced us, that fears of war were groundless. This did not diminish Gaby's faith in his powers of persuasion to obtain, from the president if necessary, a special dispensation for the exhibition of our unmade film. He was very likeable and certainly gave our importunities a veneer of sanity and reason. From week to week Gaby postponed our return to England. The fact was that he was relishing his réclame as the producer of a record-breaking film, which led him mistakenly to believe that, as a tough negotiator, he was the match of Louis B. Mayer and his executive sycophants.

Cables length away, G.B.S. must have chafed at our quixotic pursuit of an ideal Mrs. Dubedat while little attention was being paid to casting her husband on whom the play's argument turns. Several young actors had been considered but had been found wanting. As a boy I had seen Granville Barker in the part that had been written for him, but the memory of him had been eclipsed by that of Eric Lewis's comic ebullience as B.B. The most convincing performance of Dubedat I had seen since on the stage was, as I have already testified, by Alan Mowbray. He had stayed in Hollywood and won the enviable status of a first-rate supporting actor, in constant demand and free from the harassments of stardom. Now, of course, he had outgrown the part. Stephen Haggard, when he played it in London, had failed to sublimate his own essential goodness in the guise of amorality—proof if needed that an actor must be aware of the brutal and angelic elements of his nature if he is to portray the conflict between them common to many great dramatic roles. While in New York we had seen Laurence Olivier as Heathcliff in a film of *Wuthering Heights*; the strength of his personality precluded his interpretation of a character devoid of moral fibre and affecting a sentimental self-esteem as an artist privileged to ignore the mores of a civilised society. So far, the most promising candidate was Richard Ainley, the son of Henry Ainley. He would, I think, have so triumphed in the part that the whole course of his life might have been changed. But I could not persuade Gaby to come to this vital decision, so our poolside sessions dragged on and sheaves of sketches came off my drawing board until the script was finished. By then the ramifications of Gaby's wheeling and deal-ing were beyond my comprehension.

Though I found Gaby's alternating moods of humility and arrogance baffling and at times suspected that some would have diagnosed him as a fantastic liar, I had witnessed proof of the authenticity of the retrospec-tions that seemed the least credible.

One day, we visited a retired M-G-M executive at his ranch in a neigh-bouring valley. Once an Irish policeman, he had sought his fortune in the film industry, made it, and retired to make room for rivals bent on making those studios a new Jerusalem and prepared to pay phenomenal compen-sation for their chauvinism. He had married a famous, but now full-blown and impoverished, diva. As chatelaine of his palatial retreat, she enjoyed his wealth and enhanced his prestige. Throughout lunch our hostess sti-fled conversation with a surge of reminiscence contralto sforzando, while her husband sat speechless with his mouth agape like a huge bullfrog.

Afterwards, he offered to show us round his stables. Once beyond the range of his wife's singing he proved an entertaining guide. For one of his productions he had imported from Vienna a string of Lipizzaner horses and brood mares. As we approached the vast hangar where they were sta-bled, he forewarned us that he could not show them off as he would have wished, since recently they had killed the Belgian cavalry officer whom he had hired to keep them up to the mark in haute école. The doors of the hangar were rolled open. A groom led out a magnificent mare, saddled and bridled, followed by another leading her foal. As they led the spirited beasts past us, Gaby clapped his hands and growled a command in a lan-guage I did not recognise. It brought the grooms to an astonished halt. Gaby was wearing a pullover, breeches, and riding boots. Chewing the cold butt of a cigar, he took the reins and mounted the equally astonished mare who, after a show of prancing protest, recognised her master. To my knowledge, Gaby had not ridden a horse during the last year and a half. But even I saw at once that he was in centaurian unity with his mount. The mare obeyed him with docile spirit as he put her through the routines of her royal schooling. The foal, wresting herself free from the groom, ca-vorted around her dam, exciting her to rear and plunge about to her rider's evident delight, together bringing to life a study by Leonardo da Vinci for some cavalry battle-piece. When Gaby finally dismounted he was amused by our dumbfounded surprise.

"*Fantastic*—you understand?" he murmured, quietly, wreathed in his boyish grin.

So the cavalry sabre in his office was not a vain property but the treasured relic of a chivalry he had for a few minutes and perhaps for the last time reenacted.

I spent as much time as I could with old friends. Bill Menzies had been in England to design and to direct Korda's production of H. G. Wells's *Shape of Things to Come*. The design he contrived of a collapsed civilisation was so horrific, and the news from Germany so like the prelude to it, that he frightened himself into seeking oblivion in alcohol. After dining with us one evening, he had found release from his tensions to such an extent that I felt I should see him safely to bed in Mount Royal, a vast apartment hotel building. He had forgotten the number of his room. So, in close embrace, we explored one tunnel-like floor after another, as I propped him up at the end of each corridor and sought whatever number he was inspired to suggest. After what seemed hours of trial and error and several altercations with angry residents roused from sleep, I left him safely bestowed in his cell-like quarters.

His experience with Korda had not been very heart-lifting. Shaking off the colossal ruins of Rome he had created for *I, Claudius*, he left for home exasperated and depressed. Not even his steadying hand had been able to prevent this extravagant fiasco. This proved, however, to be significant. While we had been collecting piecemeal a few thousand pounds to make *Pygmalion*, several insurance companies had been conned, in the hope of making substantial profits, into investing millions in building film studios and in film productions. They were now facing what, in those days, were catastrophic losses. To cover their shame and sustain their credit, the Treasury discreetly intervened. Thus, for the first time in our history, our government was forced to subsidise one of the performing arts. Now two Hungarians had put the British film industry back on its feet, enabling it to enjoy increasing prosperity as an undischarged bankrupt.

I spent many happy evenings with Bill at his home. Tired as he was after a long day's work, he was exhilarated by his complete fulfilment as a designer in his compositions for the immense canvas of *Gone With the Wind* that was now taking shape. He and the director, Vic Fleming, were old friends and partners in production, so that every sequence of the film bears the stamp of his genius.

Gaby and I watched them at work in David Selznick's comparatively small studio, where only one picture was made at a time. They were shooting the scenes in which Scarlett O'Hara was helping an old doctor in an improvised hospital in Atlanta. The set was a masterpiece—a wooden Presbyterian church, its east window shattered by shellfire, and before the altar a great field-stove was boiling water to sterilise dressings. The floor was carpeted with grey-clad and bandaged soldiers. Bill had rid himself of the restrictive supervision of Technicolor advisers, and, boldly experimenting, had made colour his servant to enhance the dramatic impact of his camera setups. Every detail was perfectly contrived.

I felt that we, in England, had much to learn from the Hollywood set-dressers and prop-boys who were encouraged to contribute ideas and, as participants, went about their work with imaginative zest.

Vivien Leigh joined us for lunch. She had snatched the part of Scarlett from under the noses of American agents promoting their own stars. It seemed so short a time ago that, after the first night of her debut as a leading actress in Max Beerbohm's *The Happy Hypocrite*, I had danced with her at a party given by the composer Dick Addinsell. I had been very conscious of her sense of destiny and the driving professional ambition that had won her this coveted engagement. In contrast, I recalled another dancing partner, Virginia Cherrill, on the night when Chaplin chose her as a novice to play the blind girl in *City Lights* and her inability to grasp what the future might hold for an actress learning her craft for months on end at the hands of the greatest master of mime in our time.

A few days later, soon after dawn, I joined Bill on a location where acres of the umber soil of California had been sprayed with red ochre to match the cotton fields of the Deep South. I watched the slight figure of Scarlett, her long, full skirt sodden knee-high by the heavy dew, stride through her scenes with a majestic bearing that must have won the admiration of any Anglophobes in the unit.

Now and again I lunched with Douglas Fairbanks at his golf club. Physically he had changed hardly at all; he could still have played the middle-aged D'Artagnan. Although we chatted about his own shadowy film projects and of the work of others, like Chaplin, with his old generous enthusiasm, the heart seemed to have gone out of him. It had indeed failed him when he parted from Mary, forsook his métier, and sought to satisfy his craving for restless change and popularity in a futile hedonism that was contrary to the philosophy and precepts that had won his election by his fellow filmmakers and the worldwide public as the sovereign figure in the celluloid world. Now he was living with his third wife in the old beach house where we had planned so many brave enterprises. "Happiness must be earned" was the motto spelt out in stars at the finale of *The Thief of Bagdad*. Neither the joyous entertainment he had given to millions of moviegoers, nor the millions of dollars that were his just reward, had earned him the happiness he deserved. A year later, he died. When we finally parted, our old friendship had been revived in the recollections of happier times.

At Pickfair I found Mary blissfully happy in her marriage to Buddy Rogers. He had partnered with her in her last silent film, *My Best Girl*, and now was a star bandleader in his own right. The Beetle was still rolling her pile, which increased in circumference like a snowball. Resigned to her retirement as an actress, she had invested profitably in all manner of commercial ventures including the then fashionable miniature golf courses. She and Douglas met uneasily at the board meetings of United Artists, where, for once, she found herself and her refractory friend Charlie allied in their determination to prevent Sam Goldwyn from gaining control—an ambition he had nursed since his first tentative intrusion into Douglas's steam bath. One afternoon she took us on a curious expedition to cast her roguish eye over the headquarters of a new firm of film agents, where one of the many relations who battened on her had found employment. The offices were housed in an imitation colonial mansion and were furnished with eighteenth-century pieces as suspect as the bonhomie of their occupants. This was the incubator from which a parasitic monster would be hatched. Within a decade it would hold most of the film and theatrical artists of America and England in fee and, without its patronage, few could hold their own. Though such agents were supposedly furthering the interests of their clients, they soon became hand in glove with the mandarins until they dominated the entertainment industry, in due course exacting from television their mounting levies. Mary, throughout her long career, had never employed an agent. As we drove back to Pickfair she did not disguise her distaste for organisations out to rob her profession of the last vestiges of dignity and independence.

Chaplin was incommunicado. He was engrossed in forging a weapon most wounding to dictators. With more courage than European politicians in thrall to Hitler and Mussolini, he had conceived a masterpiece of satirical pantomime and had broken his vow of silence in order to make devastating mockery of the Führer's fulminations at Nuremberg. As will be seen, he was doing so at no small risk of revenge by German agents and, paradoxically, being filed by the FBI as antifascist and, by innuendo, a communist. If I could have chosen one scene in the coming war in which I could have been present, it would be the one in which Hitler, alone in his private projection room, watches *The Great Dictator*. At that moment of truth, the hide of the monomaniac may have been pierced and from the wound a trickle of self-delusion may have drained away.

I was made welcome at Walt Disney's studio, where two accomplished designers who had worked with me on *The Iron Mask* were among the group of artists he had enlisted to make moving pictures in the true sense of the words. David Hall was painting the lyrical forest backgrounds for *Bambi*; Harold Miles had made the Alsatian interiors his charming contribution to *Pinocchio*. Disney was certainly the most fulfilled artist in Hollywood. Success had not cooled his boyish enthusiasms. He wore the mantle of his independence with a flourish. He alone had conceived the limitless fun and reasonable profit to be had in animating drawings that could entrance filmgoers through no human agency other than the writers,

musicians, painters, and technicians, who, with rapidly improving methods mostly of his invention, brought the art of animation to life. It was re-
freshing to meet in that celluloid society a master-craftsman realising the
concept of his lively and whimsical imagination as he indulged his flair for
experiment in a totally new medium. He was on the best of terms with his
colleagues engaged on ambitious full-length cartoons; they, in turn, like
Florentine apprentices, held in affection and respect the master who was
the mainspring of their cooperative enterprise.

Disney ran for me the penultimate sequence of *Pinocchio*. I was over-
whelmed by the design and rhythms of the floundering whale with a fire
in its belly. Before my eyes the wave of Hokusai broke, and the ensuing
surge and turbulence of blue water was worthy of his imprint. He introduced me to a German painter working on the synchronised illustration
of Igor Stravinski's *Rite of Spring*. The walls of his studio were covered
with continuity drawings depicting the processes of the Creation, the
emergence and withering of the giant mammals, and the burgeoning of
man's occupation of the earth. *Fantasia* may not have been entirely successful. But Disney and Leopold Stokowski courageously saw it through.
If, aesthetically, it was open to criticism, it gave millions of untutored
moviegoers their first emotional response to the magic of classical music.

I left the Disney asylum with a wistful envy of my fellow painters who
had found refuge in a movie-factory where they could design and draw
to their hearts content, untroubled by the lunatic intrigues and financial
frenzies that bedevilled our Shavian endeavours. Was the prevailing
mood of gaiety, innocence, and light-hearted industry an illusion? No
doubt personal rivalries and schisms in matters of aesthetic dogma were
as common as in any monastery. But I felt sure that in the last resort the
brotherhood recognised the benign authority of Abbot Walt Disney,
though it would not have occurred to him, came near to being the artist
of Tolstoy's ideal, who "tomorrow will realise that it is more important
and useful to compose a tale, a touching little song . . . or draw a picture
that will delight dozens of generations, that is, millions of children and
adults, than to create a novel symphony or painting that will enchant a
few representatives of the wealthy classes and then be forgotten forever."

Though the critical situation in Europe was seldom out of my mind, too
often I was the target for snide comments on Britain's failure to challenge
the rampaging dictators. Hollywood had become the natural sanctuary of
German-Jewish theatrical artists in the present Diaspora. Reinhardt had
mustered enough refugee players to mount a production of Schiller's
William Tell to raise funds to meet their urgent needs.

One night I found myself at dinner sitting next to the wife of an M-G-M
executive. She told me that during the day the Jews of Los Angeles had
marched through the town in protest against Chamberlain's pusillanimity.

I asked her what she meant by the "Jews of Los Angeles," remarking that ten years ago the inhabitants of California, whatever their colour or creed, were proud Americans. No doubt, she suspected me of antisemitism. Indeed, I suspected myself of incipient schizophrenia. For when I had left home, although the justice of Hitler's territorial claims was subject to debate, his systematic and abhorrent persecution of the Jews made most of us recognise that sooner or later the Nazis must be called to account. Yet, after a few weeks in an enclave effectively governed by Jews with laws and sanctions of their own contriving, I became conscious of sharing sentiments latent in the German people that Hitler and his lackeys had cruelly exploited. In a very different Hollywood to that I had known ten years before, I observed at close quarters the power politics of film dictators cynically convinced that every artist had his price and could be brought to heel as a biddable hack; I saw men and women of creative ability concentrated in office cells where, in return for inflated salaries, they accepted the mutilation of their work and, if driven to assert themselves, were disciplined by the infliction of subtle and humiliating indignities. The system was, for me, epitomised when I learned that the immaculate Lillian Gish, an actress of genius who had learned from D. W. Griffith more of the nature of cinematic art than any so-called producer, had been invited by Irving Thalbert to fulfil her contractual obligations to M-G-M by being party to a well-publicised romantic scandal that would enhance her value as a star.

Such were the forces against which Gaby was fighting a losing battle. To his credit, he rejected tempters offering him power and affluence if he would desert Shaw and sell his soul to those whose aim was to achieve global supremacy in the production and distribution of films tailored and marketed to their idea of public taste.

Fortunately, I was jolted out of my equivocation by an incident that brought the menace of Hitler into our self-centred ménage. We had been told that the Nazi Bund was active in America, but took this idea to be propaganda by the powerful Jewish lobby to ginger Roosevelt into protesting against antisemitism in Germany. One of Gaby's ubiquitous friends was the publisher George Putnam. He was known to me as the begetter of an edition of *Moby Dick*, illustrated by Rockwell Kent that, in my view, was the most perfect example of contemporary book production. Two years before, his wife, Amelia Earhart, a pioneer airwoman, had disappeared somewhere in the Pacific at the outset of an attempt to fly round the world. Her fate was still the subject of speculation and hints that sinister forces might have encompassed her death. George often dined with us, and we in turn visited his home in Hollywood. He was the very model of an American intellectual with a cosmopolitan outlook and a lively sense of humour which made him the best of company. Recently, he had published a novella, *The Man Who Killed Hitler*, written by two

Jewish authors in New York, but for good reasons published anonymously. Soon afterwards a copy of the book pierced with three bullet holes and wrapped in cellophane was left in Putnam's letterbox. The district attorney dismissed this threat as a publicity stunt to advertise the Warner Bros. film *I Was a Nazi Spy*—a potential cash crop, when Americans in their comfortable isolation would be titillated by the idea of having an enemy in their midst, as they had been by the romanticising of gangsters in the days of Prohibition.

One evening, we returned late for a dinner at which Putnam would be joining us. We found a message from his secretary urging us to get in touch with her immediately if he had not arrived. She had found the window of his garage broken, his car gone, and his hat and spectacles on the floor. Soon afterwards, a mutual friend, Rex Colt, telephoned to say he was convinced that George had been kidnapped and begged us to help him alert the police. We had good reason to consider his reaction hysterical, for he himself was still recovering from a very real shock. His secretary's ex-husband had come to his office to kill her. Before he could do so the police arrived, and in the ensuing gunfight an officer fell, shot in the stomach. When Colt tried to take his pistol and continue the battle the wounded man waved him aside.

"If there's to be any shootin' around here, I'll do it." he said.

Raising his gun he fired and shot his man, who rolled over and died. Small wonder, then, that our friend was prone to accept melodramatic violence as part of the Californian way of life.

George Putnam was found the next morning bound and gagged with sticky tape in a half-built frame house near Bakersfield, some two hundred miles away. He told us that he had been set upon as he got into his car by three men. One drove the car through the night while the other two, with George between them on the back seat, tried with dire threats to force him to betray the authors of *The Man Who Killed Hitler*. George stoutly refused to do so. His assailants lost their nerve and abandoned him. The reaction of the jaundiced press was that this was another gambit contrived to publicise the book. I had heard that tale from George immediately after he returned and while he was still in a state of nervous exaltation. Forty-eight hours later he collapsed. Harold Dearden had taught me that such would be the psychological reaction to extreme stress, and one that a layman was unlikely to affect. The patient was much restored when he received a cable from one of the authors in New York, complaining bitterly that the name of his collaborator had been disclosed by the press and insisting that his own be equally publicised.

This kidnapping was still the subject of gossip when George's life was threatened if he attended the premiere of *I Was a Nazi Spy*. As we had planned to go with him we dissuaded him from taking further risks. I, for one, did not think it a sweet and noble possibility to die for the Warner Bros. in their gangster-ridden country.

The denouement of the farce that Gaby was unwittingly playing out was sudden and finite. He had persuaded himself that the apparent double-dealing by M-G-M was due to Mayer's absence in New York. Mayer, on his return, gave Gaby an audience of two hours in duration and dissembled so adroitly that his victim was persuaded that all misunderstandings had been resolved and that earlier promises, particularly the lease of Greer Garson that had inspired our journey, would be fulfilled. Our mediator with the State Department was so impressed by Gaby's account of the interview that he left at once for England. The brisk exchange of terse and prolix calls between G.B.S. and Gaby, together with the latter's growing conviction that he was possessed of serpentine subtlety and wisdom as a negotiator, may have impelled our mediator to find out for himself the limits of Shaw's patience and patronage, and the extent to which Pascal had committed himself to Wardour Street in return for its rescue operation in *Pygmalion*. Soon after he left us, Gaby was informed by underlings at M-G-M that the Medical Association of the United States had condemned the play as derogatory to their calling and would use every means in their power to prevent the exhibition of the film. Gaby was distraught. He showed signs of losing his head, for his self-control was as erratic as his command of the English language. Neither prevented him from invoking curses, as he stood "nakkid" by our pool, on the tribes of Israel in stentorian tones that must have reached the ears of neighbours ready to denounce him. He began to clutch at other straws in the haystack of the Shavian canon. He proposed to M-G-M that he should make a film starring Greer Garson of Shaw's latest play, *The Millionairess*, which had not yet been produced on the stage. I had read some of it to him when he was captive and in bed with a toothache. We had agreed that it was poor material for a film. So I listened, aghast, as he described to a plainly interested executive a plot that was a tour de force of improvisation but bore little resemblance to that of the play. If his audience ever read the play his suspicions that Gaby was either a rogue or a lunatic would be confirmed.

We agreed that we must cut our now considerable losses and beat a hasty retreat in the face of growing hostility fanned by Gaby's reckless anathemas that would have been applauded by the Nazi Bund. I, too, innocently enhanced our reputation as undesirable aliens. Some time ago I had been asked to speak at a banquet to be given by the American Institute of Cinematography at the University of Southern California. I proposed to review the changes in the Hollywood scene since my first visit ten years ago. I was no glib orator. I had to write my speech and learn it by heart. I imagined my audience to be as august and polite as one might expect at Oxford or Cambridge. My theme was the swindling of private

enterprise in the movie industry. For, with the exception of Chaplin, no
player or director had the independence that the founding members of
United Artists had once enjoyed. Alone in his original and fascinating
field, Walt Disney maintained the artist's sturdy autonomy, having confounded the misgivings of his own timid colleagues with the success of
Snow White and the Seven Dwarfs.

So, on the eve of my departure, I was received in the foyer of USC by
the dean who bore a comical resemblance to Leacock's Dr. Boomer of Plutoria University—curly but elegantly barbered grey hair, pince-nez on the
end of a black ribbon, a flowing gown, and an aura of spurious geniality
that did not put me at my ease. Then, to my dismay, I discovered that the
occasion was not academic but a "ladies night" and that among my fellow
guests were staunch upholders of the Hollywood establishment, including one of the Warner Brothers. What I had to say would be regarded as
in bad taste; my defence of what I called private enterprise would throw
the audience off balance, cheated of their normal response to criticism as
being liberal or left-wing and as suspect as Roosevelt's New Deal. But I
had to go through with this. Fortunately, the other oration of the evening
would be delivered by Walt Disney. Happily, we were neighbours at dinner. I confessed my coming ineptitude. He was vastly amused and relished my impertinence and, while sharing my views, promised to drag a
red herring across the trail of resentment I was bound to excite. He was
utterly faithful. He confessed, with a mocking show of bashfulness, his
wonder at being honoured by such a faculty of distinguished scholars.
His scholastic career was evidently the reverse of common practice. Being
totally uneducated, he hoped that the honorary degree the university had
bestowed upon him would lead, if he lived long enough, to his graduat-
ing from sixth grade. My gaffe was momentarily forgotten in the laughter
and applause he had invoked, until with cool farewells Dr. Boomer
speeded his uncomfortable guest off the campus. Next day a columnist of
the *Hollywood Reporter* suggested that I had overstayed my welcome.

I had planned to stay with Kathleen Norris and her husband at their
home in Sacramento on my way to New York. Gaby shrank from returning to G.B.S. empty-handed. He begged me to write a scenario of *Major
Barbara* that might incline "the Old Pope" to agree to its immediate production. Reluctantly, I agreed to do so. A most efficient secretary with her
own car was engaged to drive me up the Great Sur Way that fringed the
superb coastline. At each stopping place we worked far into the night and
the early hours of the morning. I attempted to compose action sequences
to enliven long passages of dialogue that, however brilliant, would make
filmgoers restless and inattentive. At our last port of call, Santa Cruz, the
job was done. Though Gaby was delighted by my ruthless immobilisation
of the play's static scenes, G.B.S. was not. His mimic wrath fell upon me.

"Laurence Irving must have been drunk when he wrote it," he roundly declared as he threw "the stuff" into his wastepaper basket. He was particularly scornful of my translation of Undershaft's nocturnal temptation of Adolphus Cusin to a sybaritic nightclub, but he did not veto my setting of the confrontation between Bull Walker and Major Barbara in and around a riverside pub modeled on the Prospect of Whitby in Rotherhithe.

I was happy to draw Shaw's fire and so to leave his abiding faith in Gaby unshaken. I had purposely given his play shock treatment. If I had prepared the dramatist to accept less drastic pictorial continuity essential to its adaptation to the screen, the nine days wonder of its completion was not in vain.

From Kathleen Norris I learned a lesson that in the months ahead would be ever in my mind. As a grandmother, she doted on and was deeply loved by her children and grandchildren. Her novels told of her compassion for young people and of the ups and downs of happy family life. The home she had made for them all to return to whenever they liked was gay and welcoming. Now its serenity and security was threatened by storm clouds coming up on the eastern horizon. She confided to me her fears for the future and her resentment of the intrusion of violence on her peaceful continent. For the first time I understood why so may Americans were implacably hostile to their country's involvement in the troublesome affairs of Europe. Her mother, an Irish immigrant, had crossed the New World painfully and slowly in a covered wagon and had taught her children to believe that the barrier of distance would protect them from contagion of war. Now, one of her daughter's sons was fighting with the Spanish republicans and, therefore, to his grandmother's distress, against the champions of the faith her ancestors for generations had professed. She feared to see her family sacrifice themselves for causes utterly remote from their native duty and responsibility.

Thereafter, at home, I found myself constantly defending the apparent indifference of the American people to the plight of Europe. We exchanged letters regularly until I had to tell her that, hard-pressed as we became by redskins on the warpath, I had to join those who were manning the stockade. I did not hear from her again until she knew I had lain down my arms, such as they were, and was once again practising the arts of peace.

TEN

I returned to a new home to which Rosalind had moved us in my absence. The promise of long-term work in the filming of Shaw's plays at Pinewood Studios, and the impossibility of commuting from Whitstable, compelled us to rent out our Windmill and to seek a more convenient base elsewhere.

My sister Elizabeth and her husband, Sir Felix Brunner, had recently made their home at Greys Court, near Henley-on-Thames—a perfectly situated, once fortified manor house with its ruined tower and curtain walls amid acres of poor flinty soil in which, however, magnificent trees planted by capable squires during centuries of occupation flourished in picturesque variety. The previous lady of the manor was Mrs. Valentine Fleming, the most beautiful of all the "darling mums" that the schoolmaster, Tom Pellatt, had gallantly exercised on the esplanades of Swanage as he bore passionate witness to the educational progress of her four boys in his care. Her eldest son Peter now farmed the land adjoining the beech woods of Greys Court to the westward. He was a travel writer, who, when not a-roving in the Far East, was inspiring in Geoffrey Dawson, the editor of *The Times*, the foolish fancy that he might be his successor—foolish, for he should have perceived that Peter's maverick and adventurous spirit could not endure confinement of any kind.

I and my family were offered temporary refuge in the Dower House incorporating one of the towers that in the Middle Ages had dominated the approaches to the enclave. We joyfully accepted this timely and kindly proposal, not only on practical grounds, but because our children would enjoy the company of their four Brunner boy cousins. Though no apocalyptic vision had prompted our exodus from Kent, as things turned out, it appeared to have been ordained by a guardian angel.

Meanwhile, I had been much heartened to hear that in my absence I had been elected to the Faculty of Royal Designers for Industry in recognition of my work as a film designer. This honour was doubly welcome because it was a totally unexpected tribute by fellow designers in more reputable industries who had recognised graphic design as an important component of filmmaking.

The Faculty had been created by the Royal Society of Arts to celebrate its bold attempt to promote a closer association between art and industry. In 1935 the Royal Academy, albeit nervously, put their galleries at the disposal of industrial designers to make a practical demonstration of their skills. This encouraged manufacturers of consumer goods, traditionally reluctant to improve the design of their products as long as they remained profitably marketable, to avail themselves of the talents of the increasing number of graduates from our colleges of art and polytechnics trained to apply them to industrial purposes.

I had been invited to dress a corner of that exhibition with a display of the latest British rayon fabrics. Having studied the processes of their manufacture, I symbolised their production with a white array of mechanical statuary from which flowed a rainbow stream of multicoloured material.

The president of the Royal Academy was Sir William Llewellyn, a grave and rather humourless portrait painter. He and his council had made an unprecedented and generous gesture. By statute, the Royal Academy and its schools of painting and architecture existed only to promote the practice and appreciation of the fine arts and to discourage students from applying them to less noble purposes. When the architect Sir Edwin Lutyens first took me to dine with his fellow academicians, Sir William, informally introducing me, alluded to my work as "doing scenery and that sort of thing." For a moment I felt like a prodigal son of my alma mater tasting the delicacies of her table as a welcome change from the husks that were the rations of my profession. Nevertheless, I would regret the occasion when I was the cause of bringing the wrath of his royal patron on his venerable head.

On the day before the opening of the Exhibition of Art and Industry, the Prince of Wales paid us an unexpected visit. As usual, the exhibitors and workmen were engaged in frantic last-minute activities. The prince and the president paused to inspect my creation. I could see that His Royal Highness was offended by it and heard him say so in the bluntest terms. Sir Richard, thoroughly embarrassed, approached me to suggest that I might rearrange the exhibit to look less functional, and more like a jewel on a lady's bosom. I had to tell him that, as far as I was concerned, my contrivance was immutable.

The exhibition was successful insofar as it was a declaration of our designers' intent to improve, if given the chance, the appearance, and perhaps, the efficiency of manufactured goods. It might have been more immediately effective had not the exigencies of war shifted the whole emphasis of industry and encouraged industrialists to a breach of the promise this brief flirtation with art had implied.

I found myself among the first members of a Faculty pledged to shame industry into accepting art, if not as a consort, as its handmaiden. I was delighted and amused to find that the elected apostle of theatre design was Edward Gordon Craig. The ghosts of Sir Henry Irving, Ellen Terry, and his natural father Edward Godwin were, no doubt, gratified to see their progeny thus preferred, but I hardly cared to imagine what my grandfather would have grunted on hearing the art he loved referred to as an industry.

At Pinewood I and my assistants, John Bryan and Edmund Hogan, got to work on the designs for *Major Barbara*. Shaw, although he had rejected my script treatment, gave his blessing on this substitution for *The Doctor's Dilemma*. Moreover, he gave me free hand to compose the sequences that I found most challenging—the riverside skirmishes between Bill Walker and the Salvation Army. Once again, I went on reconnaissance to the Whitechapel Road, not as before to study the apparatus of medical research but to observe at close quarters the Salvationists in the front line of their battle to rescue their fellow creatures from poverty and drunkenness. I spent two or three days with a married couple whose lives were devoted to this service. They lived in a little flat off the Mile End Road, bare of any comfortable possessions—a bivouac occupied only during the few hours they spent eating and sleeping behind the lines. Guided by this blessed pair of saints, I studied the array and deployment of their dauntless forces, their street corner sorties with banners flying and bands playing, and the shelters where their destitute captives found food, lodging, and hope.

I soon realised that the realities of the evangelism and charity I had witnessed in action bore little resemblance to the romantic caricatures drawn by G.B.S. of Barbara Undershaft and her fellow Salvationists. Was he, I wondered, always prepared to sacrifice the truth to make a theatrical occasion? I had no difficulty in portraying her father, for I took as my model Saxton Noble who, though every inch an English gentleman, was more akin to his partner Lazarus—"a gentle romantic . . . who cares for a string of quartettes and stalls at fashionable theatres." So I found myself brooding a good deal on the nature of this extraordinary man who, in his fight for overdue recognition, had teased my grandfather in order to turn the spotlight on himself and was now himself a man of such distinction that any ambitious young archer who aimed to wound him with darts of ridicule would be accused of blasphemy.

Although my acquaintance with G.B.S. was slight I had, by chance, been privileged to observe at close quarters his deportment in many of the characters he assumed, albeit with conviction, in settings that called for a variety of performances. We had a mutual friend in St. John Ervine, who consummated his lifelong devotion to G.B.S. by writing a massive, critical, and unsentimental epitaph such as he knew its subject would expect of him. St. John Ervine and I enjoyed a companionship based on frank exchanges, lively differences of opinion, and many mutual prejudices. When together, we wrestled with our self-inflicted labours in trying to portray our respective heroes clearly and dispassionately when our appraisals of their virtues and frailties was on the whole compatible. He described my grandfather as a romantic egotist and Shaw as a realistic egotist. Perhaps as two egotists, in each of whom these inclinations are equally disposed, we were qualified to referee the contention of these two stubborn champions of their respective arts.

By this time my generation venerated Shaw as a totem pole towering above his fellow dramatists with a built-in public address system that gave oracular significance to his lightest utterances. Pigmy as I was, I had been able to scan the totem at ground level from almost every aspect and had tried to reconcile its strangely disparate lineaments.

Without doubt he would be remembered as the most prolific and entertaining dramatist of the theatrical century. He could and did claim comparison with Shakespeare, though to my mind it would be as though to compare the satirical and moralising masterpiece of Hogarth with the transcendental visions of Turner. His brilliantly constructed comedies, with their characters so penetratingly drawn from life, will be applauded long after his fanciful and prolix stage debates are forgotten. He was a superb showman inviting us to walk up and take a shot at the social and political targets that we had been taught to regard as sacrosanct. He kept his audiences laughing in the theatre, but when they got home they realised that their shibboleths and comfortable complacencies had been damaged beyond repair.

I did not find him an intelligible philosopher. His reasoning could be facile and often frivolous; his premises could be puerile. His diagnosis of the morbid infections of mankind was devastating; the remedies he prescribed were merely palliative and his prognosis for the human condition fatuous. His faith in the life force had little to recommend it but the brevity of its expression.

By the time he came under my observation, G.B.S. was no longer a credible socialist. He must have learned like Tolstoy that "the aims of art are incommensurable with the aims of socialism." Certainly, as the royalties from *Pygmalion* swelled his fortune, he protested vehemently against the redistribution of his wealth by a semisocialist monarchy. The gullible old Fabian now saw the life force manifested in the messiahs Stalin, Hitler, and Mussolini.

On the platform, or wherever a captive audience was at his mercy, the actor in him, as in all Irishmen, got the upper hand. I, as my mother had been many years before, was embarrassed to hear so wise a man talking nonsense on almost any subject for the sake of getting a laugh. In one of his exhibitionist sallies he alienated the affection of his old friend and staunch champion in the theatre, Granville Barker, to his lasting regret. At his birth a mischievous fairy had endowed him with histrionic gifts that enabled him to contrive the smallest parts in his plays so perfectly as to give the players of them a lively sense of participation. At first rehearsals he would assert his ascendancy over the cast as a master mummer. His salutary advice to my Uncle Laurence and the vade mecum he wrote for the students of the Royal Academy of Dramatic Arts showed that he had a keen understanding of the technique and pitfalls of a profession to which many think they are called, but all too few are chosen to justify their pretensions.

In council at the Academy his comments and advice, particularly regarding its precarious finances, were restrained and to the point. He was attentive and courteous to his colleagues and to the principal, Kenneth Barnes, who knew how to handle him adroitly. He left his cap and bells in the lobby. Very properly this council included several distinguished actresses whose hearts governed their heads, causing them to fly off at emotional tangents. With gentle patience and engaging gallantry he would shepherd them back into the fold of reason.

When we were alone together face to face, after his diverting "cerebration" over luncheon, disputing, as I have described, an issue on which we were passionately divided, I think I saw him plain. And I remember him as a chivalrous antagonist, conciliatory and serious in reviewing our differences and expressing his opinions and generous in his unconditional surrender without a growl of the succulent bone he had gnawed for half a century.

Such then was my impression of the man of genius to whom, as it had seemed, I had now pledged my services for years to come. Content in Charlotte's care and companionship, he no longer needed or desired the consolations of friendships. He had outlived the close friends of his early middle age with the exception of St. John Ervine. He tolerated the flatterers that pressed upon him, but would have derided the posthumous eulogies in which so many of them represented themselves as the intimates they never were. Gaby's relationship to him (though he called him "the Old Pope") was that of a chaplain to an Anglican archbishop—adulatory, protective, and secure in the brief authority of his appointment.

I strove to ignore the walls of catastrophe that daily shrank the area in which artists could pursue their calling with conviction, and I was even able to persuade myself that I had graver issues to face than Hitler's menacing diatribes against Poland. Shaw and Gaby were as busily persuading themselves that, dispensing with professionals, they could assume the roles of screen playwright and director. Gaby's negotiations with James

Whale, which I had so ardently abetted, had come to nothing. Though he was an inspired coordinator of other men's talents, he lacked the power of concentration and command essential to the orderly conduct of a film studio and the time-consuming complexities of the day-to-day management of ill-assorted if enthusiastic technicians and temperamental artists. Moreover, only those closely associated with him were able to construe his blundering use of our native language. Though every line G.B.S. wrote would strike a spark of genius from the most pedestrian player, his operatic rhythm demanded a style of film cutting that dictated a tightly written script and was not to be left to haphazard "shooting" and remedial editing. Moreover, oddly enough, his visual imagination was myopic. Though, in years to come, I found his stage directions more practical and precise than those of any other dramatist, I was always astonished by his appreciative surprise of my interpretations of them, though I felt I had done no more than illustrate his clearly stated instructions.

So for the time being I concentrated on ensuring that these rogue filmmakers understood the scale, composition, and continuity of a moving picture that would be acceptable to audiences and critics. By the end of August we were sufficiently advanced to estimate roughly the cost of the film in terms of required studio space and set constructions. Thus we three ostriches buried our heads in an adaptation of *Major Barbara* for the screen, ignoring the portents of a catastrophe for which the Undershafts of this world were tooling up with keen anticipation.

EPILOGUE

On the morning of Sunday, September 3, 1939, Gabriel Pascal and I were conferring with Nicholas Davenport at his house near Farringdon. His advice and help had been indispensable to the spasmodic and at times critical financing of our film of Shaw's *Pygmalion*. Now Pascal, flushed with its phenomenal success in England and the United States, was planning to produce *Major Barbara*. At 11:15 we paused to hear Mr. Chamberlain's fateful broadcast to the nation. My heart sank as I listened to what must have been the most half-hearted declaration of a crusade in Christian memory. The prime minister's tone was sorrowful, the intrusion of his personal feeling of reluctance emasculating him as a leader. The nation, though then divided as to where its duty lay, was ready to accept whatever hardships and sacrifices the ultimate defeat of the Nazis might entail. The hearts of the people could not have been raised by that gloomy commitment to war. At the same time, Hitler and his vulgar entourage must have rubbed their hands together as they heard the feeble challenge of the only enemy they feared who evidently had no stomach for a fight.

For the rest of the month I worked with diminishing belief in the relevance of what I was doing. I became increasingly impatient with the cynical epigrams of Undershaft and the equivocations of his dependents. I hoped that, if it was not too late, the Undershafts of Great Britain were as capable as the Krupps of Germany of arming us for the coming fray.

I was depressed by the atmosphere of optimistic make-believe that persisted among well-intentioned liberals, whose convictions, hitherto, I had shared, for there would be no war on any scale and a civilised compromise would resolve our differences with Hitler, whom the Germans, their patriotic ardour cooled by our declaration of intent, would put under restraint. In *The Times* the sentiments expressed seemed designed to enervate rather than encourage the establishment. From many friends, mobilised as territorials or officers in the Supplementary Reserve, I gathered that they were chafing at the sluggish flow to their units of arms and equipment. Even when they were issued, they suggested that the coming war would begin where the previous one had ended. To my surprise, for purposes of research for shooting the industrial scenes for *Major Barbara*, I was given the run of several armament factories. With Gaby, now in the nick of time a British citizen, I watched the leisurely production of anti-aircraft guns and unimpressive-looking armoured vehicles. I welcomed the refusal of the Air Ministry to put the aircraft industry at our disposal. Perhaps, after all, we had a secret weapon up our otherwise empty sleeves.

These excursions only aggravated my personal unease. I knew that painters and scenic artists were being recruited by the War Office to revive the totally forgotten art of camouflage. Others were being commissioned as "war artists" under the leadership of the veteran Sir Muirhead Bone, who had made an incomparable graphic record of our World War I camouflage efforts. Perversely no doubt, I preferred, if I could not evade the issue, to abandon altogether the art I loved rather than to practise it in a kind of artistic purgatory. I felt it was a defeatist if necessary precaution, like the gas masks and trench digging of the Munich crisis, fostering the illusion that the hellish forces unleashed in Europe could be overcome by anything but superior force. I knew I was too old for active service. Nor could I abandon my Shavian post to sit at some paramilitary desk wearing a uniform to cloak my conscience. In my heart I think I was desperate to do something that might save my son and the sons of my friends from having to pay the price of the failure of their elders to prevent the resurgence of German militarists. So daily my despondency deepened as feverish indecision found no relief in the usually analgesic concentration on my drawing board.

My beloved wife, Rosalind, was well aware of my unease. Together we had braced ourselves to face the prospect of our children becoming embroiled in the approaching conflict. Pamela had joined the Auxiliary Territorial Service after her flight from a visit to Berlin during the Munich crisis and was now a teleprinter operator at the War Office. John had two more years to spend at Winchester College before he could fulfil his intention of becoming a pilot in the Royal Air Force. Nevertheless Rosalind, with her usual courageous and realistic approach to crises of any kind, agreed that if, thanks to my youthful experience in the RAF, I could be of service by rejoining it, I must do so. The interruption of the happiness we had shared for twenty years in such a variety of enterprises would be hard to bear, but she in turn was to find distraction from her anxieties by joining the Oxford Constabulary in which, throughout the war, she served as a typist and driver at the Henley Police Station.

Once again a chance encounter at the Garrick Club changed the course of my life. One day, arriving early for lunch, I found myself alone in the alcove below the stairs with a young barrister. He was Lionel Heald, KC, the most sought-after "silk" at the patent bar, with a thriving practice that he had abandoned to do what he conceived to be his duty in a task not only unremunerative but, as he well knew, one that was likely to be controversial. He was wearing the uniform of a flight lieutenant in the Royal Air Force Volunteer Reserve. We lunched together, and in the course of it he invited me to join him in the delicate but, he believed, very necessary commission he had undertaken at the request of the Air Council. He had been charged to form a security section of the Department of Intelligence that would be responsible for the relations between the Royal Air Force and the media, including the establishment of a system of censorship that would be acceptable to both parties. He knew of my flying service in the first war and judged that my instinctive and sympathetic understanding of problems peculiar to air warfare would be of help to him. He did not know that the shade of my godfather, Sir Edward Tyas Cook, who had been the progenitor of the censorship of the press in 1917, was hovering over us.

It did not take me long to make up my mind. My work as production designer for *Major Barbara* was done. My assistant, John Bryan, whose physical disability made it unlikely that he would be called up for active service, was capable of seeing our plans realised on the studio floor. When I asked Gaby to release me from my contract, he was at first hurt by the prospect of my desertion, but I knew that in his heart the old cavalry officer understood my discontent and he too would have made the same dutiful choice. No doubt G.B.S. declared that an Irving had once again been drunk and an easy prey to a recruiting sergeant. He had made a similar diagnosis of my condition when he read my treatment of *Major Barbara* aimed to animate his static disputations with lively action. Nevertheless, we parted on friendly terms. A few days later I presented myself at the Air Ministry, and, together with men of various ages volunteering for active service as air crew, I was commissioned as a pilot officer. So I cheerfully put the responsibility for my immediate future in Lionel's hands, not realising, perhaps, that I had committed myself in the future to serve wherever and in whatever capacity the Air Ministry might think fit.

Lionel had no difficulty in adding me to his establishment, for the Director of Intelligence at the Air Ministry was Kenneth Buss, now an Air Commodore but twenty years ago the Engineer Lieutenant RNR. upon whose skills the lives of the instructors and their pupils at the RNAS training station at Chingford depended. Archie Boyle, who handled the less orthodox and shadier aspects of intelligence, had appointed as his aide Evelyn Baring, an urbane banker, congenial companion, and an experienced man of the world of commerce. Between them, Heald and Baring brought to the Air Ministry a broadminded savoir-faire which, exercised with fearless discretion and uncompromising integrity, gave the Royal Air

Force, in matters of intelligence, a perspicacity that, for the time being, the other services lacked.

Soon I discovered that, since my Uncle Teddie, my mother's brother, had laid aside his blue pencil as the first and chief censor of the press at the end of the last war, his precepts and practices had been forgotten and no steps had been taken to promote mutual trust or a modus operandi for a necessary and reasonable degree of censorship understanding between the services and the press. The newly created Ministry of Information was still a nebula of whirling amateur bureaucrats and publicists and remained so until it became coherent under the steadying hand of Brendan Bracken. Lionel conceived his duties as being of negative and positive significance. The sole purpose of censorship was to deny the enemy information that could be to his strategic or tactical advantage. The higher aim of "security," as he saw it, was to establish such confidence between the press and those fighting the war that the latter, trusting that "off-the-record" information would be respected as such, could, when occasion arose, count upon the press and BBC to play their part in operational planning and so invigorate our embattled people in spirit and in truth.

Before the year ended three incidents had justified our existence, proved the efficacy of our method, and epitomised the variety of problems that almost hourly had to be resolved.

One morning we received a telephone call from an RAF intelligence officer in Yorkshire reporting that a Heinkel bomber and its crew had been forced to land intact on the moors near Scarborough. On inspecting the aircraft he discovered that the pilot had been posted from the Polish front to a Luftwaffe airfield in Northern Germany, from which he had taken off soon after his arrival on this sortie across the North Sea. Consequently he carried with him operational maps covering the whole field of German operations including a gridded chart of the North Sea. The latter, for purposes of radio interception, was a prize beyond price to those operating our defence systems. The young officer, realising it was vital that the enemy should be unaware that all this information had fallen into our hands, had kept curious sightseers at bay. With commendable courage but without authority he had confiscated several cameras and documents in their possession.

One of the major hazards of the "twilight war," as Chamberlain had called it, was the ease with which enemy agents or sympathisers could pass information to German intelligence organisations. All they had to do was to ring up the German legation in Dublin for their message to be relayed by wireless to Berlin. In this case Lionel instantly appreciated the situation and his countermove was imaginative. The vigilant officer was authorised to continue his surveillance and, if necessary, take punitive action. Meanwhile, Lionel suborned a friend of his in the House of Commons to spread, under oaths of secrecy, the news that a German bomber had been brought down on the northeast coast and that the crew had been rescued from the burning wreckage. Within two hours this confidential report had spread through both Houses and our telephone was kept busy with requests for further information. To our deep satisfaction, in the evening the German radio in its news bulletin paid fulsome tribute to the heroic pilot who had destroyed his Heinkel rather than let it fall into the hands of the enemy. The relative German codes and grid references remained unchanged throughout the critical months ahead.

By now we had been made party to the secret of radar interception and the disposition of its stations along our coasts, which, together with the possible ignorance of the enemy that our fighter aircraft mounted eight guns, would give us a measure of tactical surprise. On the rare occasions when we received the reports of air combats, Sir Henry Tizzard, the scientific adviser to the Air Staff, would visit us in the evening to analyse them for evidence that our pilots were beginning to hold their fire until this formidable armament could be used to maximum effect.

One afternoon Lionel returned from a high-level conference of the Air Staff with a serious problem on his hands. In the morning the chief of Air Staff, Sir Cyril Newall, and several of his directors had been invited to the private showing of a film, *The Lion Has Wings*, which had been hurriedly made by Korda, probably at the instigation of the Cabinet, to counter the reels of intimidating German documentaries of Luftwaffe operations being shown to diplomatic audiences in neutral countries. As the film conformed to Chamberlain's injunction that our bombing raids were to be confined to military targets, it was unlikely to impress anyone who had seen the horrific spectacle of the systematic destruction of Warsaw by German bombers. As Sir Cyril and his colleagues left the cinema they took leave of Korda with forced smiles and polite congratulations. On reaching the Air Ministry they sent immediately for Lionel and disclosed the gravity of what they had seen. One of the film's sequences was set in the operations room of a fighter station, where, from radar reports, aircraft approaching that coastal sector were plotted on a table on which our gridded chart of the North Sea was plainly visible. Not only the secret radar system, but its potential range, could be easily calculated by an enemy agent or attaché watching the film. Immediate steps were to be taken to see that this sequence was deleted.

Lionel, knowing that I was familiar with film production, asked me to go at once to the British Board of Film Censors and take whatever steps I thought fit to rectify this appalling blunder. That it should have happened was extraordinary because the Air Ministry had appointed an officer to act as technical adviser to the production. I demurred, for having made a clean break with my prewar occupations I had no wish to become involved in any way with the film industry. Firmly, he insisted that I was the only member of our staff qualified to deal with this emergency.

When I explained my business to the Secretary of the British Board of Film Censors, he was evidently embarrassed and inclined to be uncooperative. I could not, of course, go into the details of my critical mission. We ran the offending reel. The Air Staff was justified in its dismay. The censor telephoned Korda. His tone was apologetic; he seemed to be more in awe of the film producers than of the men responsible for the air defence of Great Britain. He put down the receiver and told me that no cuts could be made as prints of the film were being despatched forthwith to Latin America. I told him to speak to Korda again and to make it quite clear that I would cut out the necessary frames and see that any other prints were similarly censored. I would wait until the cutter who had worked on the film could be sent to make a neater job of it under my direction. Again over the telephone the vials of Korda's wrath were poured into the ear of the unhappy censor. To his credit he stood his ground and transmitted my ultimatum. In due course, a young American cutter arrived, and, as fellow professionals, we set to work and agreeably made cuts that in no way disturbed the continuity of the film. I like to think that I was able to disguise from him the true significance of our surgery.

These two negative exercises of our section added to Lionel's stature when soon afterwards he was faced with an opportunity to force a positive decision that would have a lasting effect on the morale of the Royal Air Force.

The haphazard security precautions at that time were exemplified by the admission of an ordinary civilian film unit to an airfield, where two squadrons of Wellington bombers were at readiness to make a long-planned attack on the Luftwaffe base on the island of Sylt. It was probably sheer chance that, on the eve of the launching of this raid, a squadron of ME 110s, formidably armed, twin-engined fighters was moved to Sylt. The cost of this operation was out of all proportion to its effect. Of the twenty-four Wellingtons only twelve returned to their base. As the signals came in, Lionel and I were summoned to the room of the Secretary of State for Air. There we found in conference Sir Cyril Newall, Sir Arthur Street, the Permanent Under Secretary, Air Marshal Joubert, and our own Air Commodore Buss. Sir Kingsley Wood sat back in the chair at his huge desk; his sharp, suspicious eyes behind glinting spectacles made me feel that his only concern was to emerge from the disastrous affair with his political reputation unscathed. How could the communiqué, which Lionel and I would have to compose, be worded so that the best could be made of a tactical blunder and our losses concealed. Newall was plainly out of his depth, appalled by the implications of this defeat. Joubert was calm and ready to give forceful support to a decision reached on sound principles.

Lionel declared that there were two alternatives—to tell the truth or to conceal it. If we took the latter course, the Air Ministry would never again be trusted by pilots and aircrews, who sooner or later would come to know our losses. He argued for the truth, with conviction and forceful presentation of his case, as a skilled advocate. I could do no more, as his junior, than endorse his far-sighted wisdom. Newall rose from his chair and went alone into an adjoining room. In his absence we reexamined the available evidence. Of the twelve Wellingtons missing, five had been making for Holland streaming clouds of petrol vapour and trails of smoke. Their ultimate fate would not be known to the enemy for some time. Newall rejoined us. For a minute or two he sat with his head in his hands. Then, taking the whole burden of decision on himself, he said: "You will say that seven of our aircraft are unaccounted for."

This half truth was, we agreed, justified in this case. But Lionel had established a long-term policy that, harsh though it seemed, assured the trust of the Royal Air Force, the people of Britain, neutral observers, and oppressed Europeans listening secretly to BBC news bulletins in the accurate reporting, favourable or unfavourable, of our casualties in the great air battles to come. That conference was memorable for me for it was my first meeting with Sir Arthur Street. Later I would have to disturb this patient and devoted civil servant at all hours of day and night. Some future historian, with access to all the documents relating to the preparation of the Royal Air Force for its coming ordeal, may discover him as the Samuel Pepys of our time, who wore himself out in realising his vision on which the survival of our nation would depend.

My first confrontation with the press led me to suppose that journalists could be treated as responsible professionals to whom the truth could be confided and by whom the suppression of news in the exigencies of war would be accepted.

Winter came early that year with sharp frosts and heavy falls of snow. We had the weather gauge of the enemy for as a rule most depressions and anticyclones approached Europe from the West across the Atlantic. So, at the outbreak of war, meteorological reports ceased to be published, leaving the enemy to make the best forecasts they could from intermittent reports from their long-range aircraft and submarines.

The war had not dampened the British enthusiasm for sport. If league football matches had to be abandoned owing to water-logged or snow-bound playing fields, the public would expect the sporting columns of the press to forewarn them. One afternoon I found myself facing the assembled editors and deputy editors of Fleet Street. Hesitantly, for I was truly unaccustomed to public speaking, I explained that any indication of the state of football grounds would enable the enemy to deduce the condition of our airfields and the effect of the weather on their operational state of readiness. My audience listened attentively, asked only a few questions, and assured me that they could be relied upon not to mention the weather in relation to any sporting fixtures. Afterwards several editors thanked me for my briefing. This became common practice, and they accepted similar censorship as a necessary restriction in time of war.

As 1939 drew to a close Londoners fell into an optimistic apathy. Like children playing hide and seek in a shrubbery, they accepted the blackout as an inconvenience that hid them from bombers seeking to destroy them. The Nazis were no more anxious than we were to provoke retaliation for the time being.

One day I met Ben Travers. I soon discovered that he, far nearer retirement as a warrior than myself, felt that there was no future for the arts until, one way or another, the fate of our civilisation was determined. I suggested that he join us in A.I.6. Temperamentally he was perfectly equipped to cope with the problems that by now were our daily portion. His genial patience and impatience with fools or humbugs would reinforce our skirmishes with obtuse members of the Air Staff and restive journalists, making them see reason in our importunity and on occasion laugh at themselves. Again our director welcomed an old friend into the fold, for the rather ghostly figure of Ben loomed in a photograph of his fellow staff officers at Chingford in 1918 that stood upon his mantle. Our office was now a congenial annex to the Garrick Club.

Most of our colleagues lived in London and were fathers of young families. So Ben and I, our homes being in the country, volunteered to hold our beleaguered Air Ministry fort of censorship over Christmas. Both of us believed in our hearts that the joy of our youthful hopes was ended and that those years we romped through in the fields of opportunity were but a brief period of mankind's convalescence between recurring fits of international violence. We shared the tacit understanding that the resumption of our careers became daily more remote. Yet as the Westminster chimes of Big Ben heralded another birthday of the Prince of Peace, as we lay on our truckle beds within reach of our battery of telephones, "we wrapped our martial cloaks around us and laughed ourselves to sleep."

INDEX

131